THE
CHRISTIAN
OF THE FUTURE

ABOUT THE BOOK

The Christian of the Future is a reflection on the nature, limits, and possibilities of change taking place in the Church during and since the Second Vatican Council. The opening chapter, on "The Changing Church," seeks on the one hand to warn against the hazards of naïve progressivism, and on the other hand to search out efficient neoteric methods of effecting change. This is followed by two essays on the scope and direction of future dialogue between the Church and secular organizations, and on the qualifications of the Church in the public social sphere. The last part of the book is a kind of preview of the post-conciliar epoch, an attempt to formulate, from among the work of the Council, those truths which will provide especial sustenance for the Christian of tomorrow.

QUAESTIONES DISPUTATAE

KARL RAHNER

THE
CHRISTIAN
OF THE FUTURE

HERDER AND HERDER

1967

HERDER AND HERDER NEW YORK

232 Madison Avenue, New York, N.Y. 10016

This book is a translation of the following four chapters of "Schriften zur Theologie", vol. VI, published by Benziger Verlag, Einsiedeln, Zurich, Cologne, 1965: 'Kirche im Wandel', 'Zur "Situationsethik" aus ökumenischer Sicht', 'Grenzen der Amtskirche' and 'Konziliare Lehre der Kirche und künftige Wirklichkeit christlichen Lebens'. Translated by W. J. O'HARA.

Nihil Obstat: Joannes S. Coventry, S.J.
                 Censor deputatus.

Imprimatur: ✠Patritius Casey, Vic. Gen.

Westmonasterii, die 5ª Septembris, 1966.

Library of Congress Catalog Card Number: 66–28290

First published in West Germany © 1967 Herder KG
Printed in the Republic of Ireland by Cahill & Co., Ltd.

CONTENTS

PREFACE

This collection of essays has ensued from the author's reflections on the situation of the Church in the conciliar and post-conciliar period. The first essay, "The Changing Church", offers some thoughts on the limits of change within the self-understanding of the Catholic Church. It seeks not merely to warn against a falsely understood "progressism", but, with the same decisiveness, to arouse courage to discover new and bold ways in the Church of God. In view of the ecumenical efforts of the present, the author depicts, in the second essay, by means of the example of "situation ethics", the course which he envisages for a present-day ecumenical dialogue. The opening of the Church to the world calls for a whole series of fundamental debates on the limits of the possibilities of the Church for coping with secular situations of a private and social character. The third essay, "The Church's Limits", sketches the author's thoughts above all on the capacity of the Church to give directions in the public social sphere. The last part of the book attempts a preview of the post-conciliar epoch: which of the teachings of the Constitution on the Church will especially have to touch the heart of the future Christian, if he is to live his faith in the world of tomorrow?

These questions form, in a way, only an accidental selection out of the countless problems posed by the Council documents.

7

They are not a commentary but an elucidation of some of the focal points of the conciliar *event*, which perhaps did not even find much expression in the official promulgations. Some of it is an elaboration of thoughts which just crossed the author's mind and an attempt to draw them generally into consciousness. However, all these reflections seek to help prepare a little the path of the pilgrim Church, so that even in our time it may proclaim and mediate the grace of God.

The original German version of these essays, which are the texts of various lectures given by the author (see note at the end of the book), has appeared in the sixth volume of *Schriften zur Theologie* (1965). The author and the publishers are grateful to Dr. Oscar Bettschart, Director of Benziger Verlag, Einsiedeln, for permission to publish their English translation in the *Quaestiones disputatae* series.

Karl Rahner

Munich,
July 1966.

THE CHANGING CHURCH

There is no doubt that the Second Vatican Council, its proceedings and debates, the differences of opinion that became apparent, the press reports that retailed and exaggerated them, the existence of tendencies and parties thus revealed, the struggle for decisions this way and that, the alterations in liturgy and law decided upon—all these experiences caused profound astonishment, disquiet and consternation in many Catholic circles, even to a considerable extent among the clergy. The remark, falsely attributed to a conservative cardinal, that he would still like to die a Catholic, is merely a slight, odd symptom. Other Catholics greeted the Council and its work enthusiastically as the long-awaited and already really overdue *apertura*, throwing open the Church's windows to let in some fresh air, and as a rebuilding of the old fortress with its narrow loopholes into a house, equally strong but with broad glass walls and the world shining in through them, and at most thought the tempo and results still much too modest. But the first had an inescapable impression of profound alarm.

Their previous experience had shown them the Church as an unshakable tower in the seething waves of time—*stat crux dum volvitur orbis*—as the only authority with the courage to hold unalterable principles, as the herald of eternal granite-firm dogma, of enduring natural law, of venerable tradition

9

unquestioningly accepted and lived, of clear-cut Yes and No, of plain principles which are always known from the start and only need fearlessly to be put into practice, whether the world approves or not. To them precisely the unshakable immutability of the Church's doctrine and life seemed a decisive characteristic of the Catholic Church in contrast both to other Christian denominations and to the spirit of the age generally. And now they have the impression that people are discussing anything and everything, questioning everything, that everything is collapsing, that their own perhaps hard-earned and dearly-bought rigid adherence to the doctrine, and above all the traditional practice, of the Church even to the slightest concrete detail of the style of religious and secular life, is disavowed and almost despised by the Church and its leading representatives. The bitter feeling of being left in the lurch by the Church, of standing as an object of reproach before the eyes of the world of non-Catholics "who always knew it", temptations against faith, mistrust of the reliability and trustworthiness of ecclesiastical authorities, such are the consequences of "Council experiences" of this kind which in fact—there is no doubt about this—have rightly or wrongly been undergone by many Catholics.

It is not necessary to illustrate this situation here at the beginning of our reflections with particular examples of the questions or proceedings which gave rise to disquiet, since we shall have to go into the matter, as far as is necessary and possible, when forming a judgment on it.

The situation in question should be clear enough already. It is the state of those who ecclesiastically are conservative in face of the experience of profound changes in the Church.

And in this context the word "conservative" means in principle something quite positive, for it also includes the courage to affirm continuity, clear principles, detachment from ephemeral fashions, fidelity to the Word of God which endures for ever, respect for tradition, for what has organically developed, for the wisdom and experience of our ancestors.

What is to be said of this state of affairs? What has the Council taught, decided, done in this respect, and what has it not taught, decided, done? What is to be said regarding mutability and immutability in the Church's doctrine and in Christian morals and life? That is the question with which we shall be concerned here. We are not concerned with the manifold changes in the Church which form the main theme of Church history, in other words changes which are simply imposed on the Church as an inevitable consequence of the Church's insertion in a total pattern of historically operative forces (State, civilization etc.). We are concerned with the change which the Church itself actively undertakes in its law and doctrine, and in which the Church changes itself, and is not merely subjected to change, though of course both sets of changes mutually affect one another.

In order to make some advance in the obscurity and complexity of the question, and to provide a guiding line for our reflections, a distinction must first be drawn, even though we cannot but realize that the two poles of the distinction are linked by manifold connections of the most complicated kind. We refer to the distinction between ecclesiastically binding and, in the strictest case, dogmatically defined teaching of the Church on the one hand, and Church law and the actual living practice of the Church on the other. Let us assume for the moment this distinction as valid and important and its meaning as understood. It will follow as a matter of course from what we are about to say, and will be seen to be necessary and profoundly justified.

Changes in the law of the Church

That distinction being presupposed, let us first ask what is to be said on the question of mutability or immutability of canon law and the Catholic style of life bound up with it, if we may so describe all the practices, rules, modes of behaviour in a Catholic's church life and his secular life lived on Christian lines, which hold good or previously held good through education, church precept etc. On occasion these go beyond the strict rules of law, but to a certain extent constitute their expression in everyday concrete terms, their practical realization. What we mean by canon law in relation to the present problem is plain, but merely for the sake of clarity, and making an arbitrary choice, I list a few examples without system or order of importance: Friday abstinence, the law of fasting, the rules for the eucharistic fast, the law regarding the form of contracting marriage which alone is valid in normal circumstances for the Catholic, his duty of yearly confession and Easter Communion, the precept of burying the dead in the earth, the prohibition in certain circumstances from joining certain political parties, the rules of the Index of prohibited books, the regulations concerning church collections (cf. the Church tax in Germany), ecclesiastical procedure in matrimonial causes etc. There are very many laws of that kind and they deeply affect the life of the layman.

What is to be said of them in relation to the mutability and immutability of the Church?

In the first place, the difference and the connection between divine law and positive Church law must be considered. The first is unchangeable, either because it is law which flows from the absolutely immutable nature of God and man, or because it is law which promulgates God's revelation as the divine will for the whole Christian era of grace and Church. Positive Church law is in principle subject to alteration and has to be changed by the Church if a new historical situation requires this. Perhaps this difference has not always been very clear to the average Christian without special theological formation, but it has always been clear to the theologian, and consequently the Christian need not be surprised that it plays a part in the Church's practice. It is of course impossible here to demonstrate with full grounds the fact that such and such a provision of canon law belongs to immutable divine law, whereas others belong merely to mutable Church law.

The general principle is, however, easy to grasp. Examples of one or other of the two kinds of divine and unchangeable law would be, that a marriage between brother and sister is now invalid independently of the will of the Church; that a validly consummated marriage between baptized persons is indissoluble and that the Church has no power to alter the fact; that the Church cannot abolish the fact that there are seven sacraments, nor alter the ultimate features of the Church's own constitution. No bishop at the Council ever called that in question. In a particular individual case it may be doubtful whether a concrete norm belongs to unchangeable divine law or to changeable human law; for example, whether,

13

"in itself", apart from the Church's law, it would be possible, after the death of his father, for a step-son to marry his father's second wife. But that makes no difference to the principle. There is immutable divine law in the Church and the Church in its clear unclouded awareness of the faith has always been conscious of the fact in regard to such fundamental laws as a whole. And it would be simply faulty theological formation, and rashness, if a Christian were to assert that because the Church can change or has changed a mutable positive Church law, it is also in a position, or obliged, to alter a law which it knows is divine and unchangeable, simply because it has a certain material affinity with mutable canon law. Though the Church can, for example, abolish certain existing prohibiting impediments to marriage, of purely ecclesiastical law, if it considers this advisable in the changed situation of today, it by no means follows that it would be equally possible for the Church to revalidate and sanction any invalid marriage whatever, if the Church were only rather more liberal and understanding.

But there is also mutable positive ecclesiastical law. It probably in fact constitutes quantitively the greater part of the rules of law binding on a Catholic. We cannot of course go more closely here into the question why the Church has the right and duty, not only to promulgate and inculcate the precepts of immutable divine law and to supervise its observance, but on its own initiative to go beyond this and lay down positive legal prescriptions, and impose obedience to them as a Christian's duty, although they are enacted with full consciousness that they are not necessarily eternally valid but can be changed and even abolished. On this point we will only remark that Christ gave his Church such a plenary power and duty because without it a common life in the Church and concrete pastoral care by the Church for the salvation of the individual would be quite impossible. And it should at once be noted also that as long as such a Church law is in existence, the character of its obligation, the possibility of being excused or dispensed from it, the possibility of discussing its expediency or the need to change it, the possibility of knowing oneself not bound by it in a particular concrete case etc., are of quite a different kind from any case in which an immutable divine commandment is involved. At all events there are such changeable ecclesiastical laws; the Church's theology was always aware of it and has always successfully endeavoured to draw a clear distinction between divine laws and Church laws and to keep it clearly in mind. That normally a Catholic's marriage has to be contracted in the presence of the priest if it is to be valid, that cremation is not usually permitted, that Communion must ordinarily be received fasting, that in a mixed marriage the non-Catholic partner too must promise that the children will be brought up as Catholics, that in the case of serious sin the sacrament of penance must be received within the year, that we must assist at Mass every Sunday, that without special permission it is forbidden to read a book on the Index, even when there is no danger to one's own faith or morals, that flesh meat may not be eaten on Fridays, that it is not permitted without special dispensation to contract marriage with a non-baptized person or with a relative within the third degree etc.—all these are, or were, not only precepts differing greatly in importance and therefore entailing very different degrees of obligation, very different possibilities of exemption and dispensation, but they all belong to positive ecclesiastical law and, as such, are susceptible of change. The Church was always clear about that. It makes no difference if some individual Christian does not know it, but regards such precepts as immutable principles of his life and then is surprised when the Church makes changes in them.

If the Church alters laws of that kind and to that extent itself changes, it does so only within the immutability of a fundamental principle, namely, that the Church has the right and duty to make changeable regulations for the spiritual good of its members. Of course the Church does not enact and alter such changing laws arbitrarily and capriciously. Moreover, the justification, expediency or inopportuneness of such change is very different from law to law. The Church ought, for example, long ago to have abolished genuflection before the Blessed Sacrament in Japan in favour of a deep bow, in deference to Japanese feelings, or to have ceased using spittle at baptism, as has now been done. But the Church is scarcely likely to abolish the obligation of confession within the year in the case of grave sin, even though this obligation only dates from 1215, for positive Church enactments of that kind, for all their alterability in principle are, after all, ultimately the concrete embodiment of the changeless precepts of the Gospel, determinate ways of carrying them out, means of making them clear. Church laws on the plane of positive human law very definitely stand in closer or remoter relation to the precepts of divine law. Consequently the possibility and tempo of their alteration are rightly different.

Change of that kind, however legitimate, and however much it was allowed for from the start in the Church's legislation, can of course lead to unrest and uncertainty in the practice of Church life, especially among the laity. Behind even a law of the Church there stands the holy authority of God, to the extent that he empowered the Church to make laws. But it validates such laws quite differently from the commandments of God which follow directly and imperatively from the essence of the natural or supernatural realities created by God himself, and which therefore were posited by the very fact of God's directly positing those realities. But in the average practice of life, the Christian is often not clearly conscious of this radical distinction. He therefore reacts to an alteration in such Church precepts almost as if God or the enduring nature of the Church had altered, and as if, as a consequence, neither of them were to be trusted any more. He becomes uncertain. He can be very disillusioned if he has observed such a law (that of burial of the dead in the earth, for example), perhaps at the cost of considerable moral efforts and personal sacrifices, and now suddenly has to see that things—if we may so express it—are all at once much easier. The only help here is patience and understanding of the fact that even the Church necessarily and in accordance with its duty has to bow to the law of history by which what was good yesterday is not good today. New epochs, the emergence and character of which are not under the Church's control, require from the Church action different from that of the past.

Such adaptations are necessary. They cannot simply always be left to the various individual and smaller units of the Church. Yet it may be that an alteration that has to be imposed universally, is urgently needed or even overdue in one place, but in another is less necessary and may even lead to disturbing or destroying still useful and well-tried institutions belonging to a traditional manner of life. Evening Mass, for example, can be an imperative requirement of attentive pastoral care in a large town, whereas in a village it may tend rather to have an adverse influence on piety of a genuinely traditional kind. Yet it may well be that a general regulation has to be laid down. It must not be overlooked either that, even in the Church, human strata coexist chronologically which sociologically, intellectually and culturally belong to quite different epochs. Yet the same law has to be laid down for all. In a new industrial district, for example, only a single church can be built for all, yet it has to be used by people of the most heterogeneous artistic taste, so that to one a crucifix may seem blasphemous which others find a most genuine expression of their religious feelings.

In earlier periods of the Church such changes in canon law and the style of Christian life could take place so slowly that the individual scarcely noticed them, his own span of life being so short, or at least they did not come as a shock to him. Nowadays the tempo of all domains of secular history is so accelerated, and the scale of intellectual, cultural and social changes has so increased, that the Church can scarcely fulfil its obligation to meet the demands of every age in any other way than by hastening and increasing the tempo and scale of its own changes in what can be changed.

When a Council sets itself a task of that kind, it is inevitable that there will be surprises, that what is dear and well-tried will be sacrificed, that experiments will be risked and innovations introduced, the ultimate consequence of which no one can foresee with certainty. In comparison with the breadth and depth of the intellectual, economic, cultural, social changes of today and tomorrow in the secular sphere, however, which also contribute to determine the task of the Church, it must even be said that the Church in its *aggiornamento* proceeds very slowly and cautiously, so that there is more reason to ask whether it is reacting sufficiently quickly, courageously and confidently to the future which has already begun, than to fear that it is sacrificing too quickly and in too "modernistic" a way what is old and well-tried and has stood the test. Of course such an alteration involves for hierarchy and rank and file an uncomfortable period of transition: the old and well-tried is no longer there; the new has not yet got into its stride, has not yet become something that is taken for granted without discussion; the intellectual and religious attitudes necessarily required if the new institutions are to succeed have first slowly to develop. Consequently it may seem as if the old were better than the new. An apparently "laxer" law regarding mixed marriages, for example, can only bear genuine fruit of a positive kind when a personal, religious, responsible mentality has grown up among Catholics in this matter. It may be that the ecumenical attitude and mentality now officially adopted by the Church will lead to a decrease in the number of conversions, at least temporarily, or lead in some cases to indifference in regard to the denominational question. And yet such ecumenism is a sacred imperative of our age.

Such periods of transition have to be endured with patience and courage and without morbid nervousness. It must be calmly realized that every reconstruction, even the most necessary, produces discomfort and raises a lot of dust. It must be soberly realized that no human enactment, whether old or new, has advantages only and no disadvantages; that the old days were good only for those who enjoyed the benefits of them, but not for all without distinction and that for the most part they only begin to look splendid when they are past and gone; that even the new age will produce tribulation, inadequacies and defects, and that the reform of the Church is never at an end. Nor is it the case that every well-meant alteration in the human law of the Church or in its para-canonical mode of life (which is often even more important than canon law itself) necessarily achieves the sole correct solution by the mere fact that it is well-considered and well-meant. It is still possible to remain divided in opinion, for example, about the right age for Confirmation or first Confession, even if the Church has laid down some definite practice with greater or less binding force. In short, anyone who appreciates the rapid change in historical circumstances and does not flee from this into a ghetto; anyone who knows that there is and always has been a mutable, human law of the Church, and that this kind of change has always been practised; anyone, moreover, who reflects that the Church not only has the right but the duty of shaping its canon law in accordance with changes in the times, will not be surprised at the change in many legal regulations which he is living through at the present time, but will recognize and accept this as a sign of the vitality of the Church and its pastoral care. He will recognize in the change itself the immutable which would itself be betrayed by rigid immutability: fidelity to the eternal Gospel and obedience to the Lord of history, which both go to produce the change in the Church's legislation.

We said at the beginning of our reflections that we must distinguish between ecclesiastically binding (and in the strictest case dogmatically defined) doctrine on the one hand, and canon law and the living practice of the Church on the other. We also stressed that despite this necessary distinction, there are close relations between the two. This affirmation can now be grasped more precisely. To the extent that in canon law there are maxims which belong to divine, immutable law and derive from the essence of natural or supernatural realities, they also belong to the Church's doctrine of faith, to its dogma. Consequently what will have to be said in a moment regarding the mutability and immutability of the Church's doctrine of faith applies to them. Yet to the extent that canon law contains mutable human positive law enacted by the Church itself, it forms an object in itself distinct even materially from the Church's doctrine, and which as such is not directly the object of the Church's teaching authority and of faith, but of the Church's jurisdiction, of obedience, of considerations of expediency etc. It follows that the principles of change and permanence for this kind of ecclesiastical law are different from those which govern the Church's doctrine of faith.

The mutable element in the doctrine of faith

This brings us to the question of change and immutability in the Church's doctrine. In this connection it must be clearly realized from the start that the belief of the Church, the object of its teaching office, contains both statements about divine realities such as the blessed Trinity, the Incarnation of the Logos, grace, redemption etc., and equally clear and equally obligatory statements about man's correct moral principles. "Murder is a sin" is just as much a proposition of faith as "there are three persons in God". It must not be overlooked that the most disturbing question regarding the immutability of the Church's doctrine of faith has been raised very recently by a real or supposed change in the Church's moral teaching, in moral theology, especially in regard to sexuality. What is to be said of the immutability and mutability of the Church's doctrine?

In the first place it can be taken as axiomatic in the Catholic view of faith that where the Church's magisterium has once unambiguously required at any time an absolute, ultimate and unconditional assent of faith to a definite doctrine as revealed by God, the doctrine in question is no longer subject to revision and is irrevocable. This is so even if previously, in earlier times, it had not been taught with the same absolute requirement of belief. It may even have been controverted, though this does not of course mean that the Church ever taught the contrary as absolutely binding. Such a dogma of the Church is truly unchangeable, i.e., it can never cease, even by an act of the Church, to be binding on the conscience of the Catholic. Only journalists very badly instructed in theology could therefore suppose that Vatican II might cancel the doctrine defined by Vatican I regarding the papal primacy of jurisdiction and teaching authority, or out of ecumenical spirit and desire to please, might revoke the dogma of the Immaculate Conception or the Assumption of the Blessed Virgin Mary. Nothing of the kind ever entered the head of a single bishop at Vatican II, even among the most progressive. There was never a discussion in the Theological Commission or in the full assembly of the Council which implied any such supposition. But the immutability of the Church's dogma does not exclude, on the contrary it implies, that there is a history of dogmas. Such a history does not only exist because a very great deal of time and theological development and clarification was needed in some cases before the Church's awareness of its belief had finally fought its way to a clear realization that such and such a definite doctrine of the Church is really contained in divine revelation, is a genuine expression of what has always been globally believed or an obligatory defence against heretical misinterpretation of what has been handed down.

There is a legitimate history of dogma also where a dogma is already unmistakably present and expressed. For even the meaning of a dogma of this kind can be thought out still further, more profoundly clarified; freed from misunderstandings which spontaneously accompany it and which earlier times cannot have been conscious of; brought into more explicit connection with other truths of faith. And by all this the meaning and limits, scope and significance of the dogma become clearer. It can be expressed in new formulations which the spirit of a new age suggests and which place it in quite different perspectives which make it intellectually more assimilable to men of a new age. In ecumenical discussion with non-Catholics it can be expressed in a new way so that these Christians may more readily recognize its compatibility with those Christian truths which they hold as the core of their own position as Christians.

In these and other respects even the Church's unchangeable dogma can have a history and can change even in spite of its immutability. It cannot change back, it cannot be abolished (like a positive ecclesiastical law). But it can change forwards in the direction of the fullness of its own meaning and unity with the one faith in its totality and its ultimate grounds. In that case it resembles a man who remains true to himself and his nature and the law according to which he has first begun, who becomes identified more and more completely with his origin, expresses his enduring nature more and more, and in that way changes and yet remains precisely the same man. There is no doubt that in this sense there was a development of dogma at the Second Vatican Council. But no old dogma was abrogated or even obscured. Undoubtedly a certain insight was promoted in regard to such questions as how the papal primacy and the episcopacy founded by Christ can exist and work together in the Church, how the necessity of the Church for salvation is compatible with the possibility of salvation of a human being who does not belong to it, how in the realm of grace each of the regenerate can depend on every other and so above all on Mary, while there is nevertheless only one mediator between God and man, Jesus Christ. Development of dogma took place in these matters without prejudice to existing dogma.

Of course this can involve quite considerable changes in the individual's understanding of the faith. Anyone who previously had unthinkingly understood the dogma of the primacy of the pope as meaning that the bishops were only subordinate, provincial papal officials, was given a fundamental lesson by Vatican II. But his previous conception of the dogma of the primacy was a misunderstanding, not a dogma that had to be annulled. Naturally such a change can also have incalculable ecumenical importance because even Catholic theology cannot foresee all that is still possible in this sense and in this direction. Otherwise this part of the history of dogma would already be over. And no one should say beforehand that future change of this kind (the validity of existing Catholic dogma remaining unaltered) would not be sufficient to restore unity of belief among all Christians. For such change within the unchanging identity of the one enduring dogma can be very extensive indeed. It can exhibit the "old" dogma from quite a different angle, and profoundly alter the concrete form in which it appears in the thought and especially in the life of the Church. We profess, for example, the dogma of original sin to this day, with Augustine; it was defined as a dogma in his time. Yet what an alteration this enduring dogma has undergone in regard to its more precise formulation, its more exact theological interpretation, its perspectives, the consequences that are to be drawn from it, the weight it has in religious life. That would have to be demonstrated in detail in order to give those untrained in theology some idea of what development even an actually defined dogma can still undergo, without being abrogated and without its original sense ceasing to be guaranteed. This sort of thing can be seen retrospectively from a later point in history but can at the most be guessed at from an earlier one. God's truth remains the same, yet it is living and has always a history which will only come to an end in the vision of God. Until then even the enduring, permanently valid truth is only partial, spoken in images and parables, wandering and therefore changing on the pilgrim road of unpredictable history.

For life within the Catholic Church, the stumbling-block as

regards change in the Church's doctrine is not so much the question of defined dogmas as other doctrines of the Church in dogmatic and moral theology which are taught authoritatively but which in principle cannot count as defined doctrines of faith or as irreformable dogma.

Non-defined doctrines

In the first place it should be recalled that there is and must be doctrine of that kind. Even the concrete knowledge of truth which a human being possesses cannot be confronted with the alternative either of affirming a proposition with ultimate unconditional certainty and determination or of abandoning it as absolutely uncertain and without obligation. In their life and reflection, human beings possess various items of knowledge which, though they lack the ultimate degree of clarity, certainty and obligation of a theoretical and moral kind, yet are and must be valid for them, at least until they attain better insight. So it is with the Church. Its teaching is not, of course, the small sum-total of a few isolated, ready-made propositions which simply stand side by side like the ultimate axioms of geometry. Its doctrine expresses the one unfathomable mystery of God, of his presence in Christ, of grace and of the permeation of the immensity of human existence by this absolute communication of God. Such a doctrine is necessarily of incalculable multiplicity. It is always present in its entirety as an unanalysed whole of inexhaustible depth and breadth. At the same time it is involved in the history of the Church's faith. It possesses in its elements and their interrelations innumerable cross-links, connections, aspects. It presents ever-new facets when in the course of the intellectual history of mankind it is confronted with ever-new human experiences, because it points to the infinite mystery of God as the centre of our own existence.

Such a doctrine cannot be presented with the alternative either of enunciating on all occasions what is absolutely binding or of saying nothing at all. It is not possible to state the propositions of actual dogmas themselves without expounding them, elucidating the terms employed in them, establishing connections, offering aids to their understanding etc. Without all that, which is not itself dogma, the dogmas themselves would be unintelligible and as regards faith no longer assimilable by the hearer. But if that is done by the Church's magisterium, it can only be through propositions which are not themselves absolute dogma but serious and valid items of knowledge (in varying degrees, of course, and of very many different kinds), but knowledge which in principle is subject to revision and capable of improvement, and which can be deepened, clarified, given greater discrimination, improved in this or that respect, or even abandoned. If such propositions are put forward by the magisterium itself, they require respect and assent from the individual believer. He must regard them as the at present available and binding ways of access, as elucidation, as props to understanding the dogma of the Church relating to salvation. He can and must do so, even if he is neither entitled nor obliged to give the same kind and degree of assent to such doctrine as to actual dogmas, because genuine internal assent and the irrevocable assent of faith are not the same thing.

Such propositions of the Church's magisterium and of

theology (derived from the former or preparing them) exist above all in the sphere of moral theology. For here it is a matter of the application of the ultimate fundamental attitudes and doctrines of the Gospel to the unimaginable multiplicity of situations in human life which, moreover, are involved in a perpetual historical flux and change. What is to be done when money slowly comes to represent productive goods, which was not always the case? Is interest then allowed, which it was not before? What morally is to be done when nuclear weapons are invented? What is morally permissible when technical physiological possibilities of birth control appear which did not exist previously? How is the danger of a possible over-population to be avoided, something which in former times was quite outside men's field of vision? How can the legal and social position of women in public life and in the Church be rightly assured as God wills it, in circumstances which 200 years ago were quite unthinkable? To such questions and many others the answer cannot simply be drawn ready-made and plain from the Gospel or from traditional teaching, because it is just not already contained there in that way and cannot be. On the other hand the Church cannot in all cases leave the individual human being to seek the answer on his own account and at his own risk. The Church in many cases (I do not say in all) must first find such an answer. The Church has to seek an answer and that requires a development, a history of reflection, time.

At such a time obscurities, oscillations, essays, a certain one-sidedness, are unavoidable. That is easily observed for example in the period of transition from a feudal authoritative state and a society with a closed mental outlook, to a democratic, pluralist social order. From Gregory XVI to the Declaration of Vatican II on toleration, the Church travelled a long way before it could formulate its position in regard to modern society in a many-sided and to some extent mature form. That long process was needed because the reality to which the Church had to adopt an attitude was itself in movement and still is. It would be childish and unjust to think, on account of the historical character of its doctrine in such questions, that the Church says one thing one day and the opposite the next. Even where the Church is still only on the way with its own doctrine, it draws its formulas each time out of its own enduring basic convictions, which always recognizably and unchangeably shine through the attitudes and concrete formulations, which at first sight by their merely literal tenor appear different or contradictory. When, for example, at first in the 19th century down to Pius XII the Church adopted a very reserved attitude to any inclusion of the human *bios* in the idea of evolution, that was motivated, and rightly so, by a fundamental conception of the nature of man which for good reasons required to be defended. That fundamental view is still that of the Church now, but it has been recognized that the previous reserve can be abandoned. To affirm that in this way a necessary, unavoidable, historical process of development on a large scale in the doctrines which are not defined dogma is legitimate and a matter of course, is not to say that this history does not also contain mistakes, over-hasty (though only provisional and revocable) decisions, cases of short-sightedness and lack of understanding. Such things can and will happen. They too belong to the Church's figure as a servant and a pilgrim, which must be patiently borne by its members.

There exists, therefore, and must exist, a teaching of the Church which possesses an importance and binding force for the faith and moral conscience of the individual Catholic, although in what it directly states it cannot and does not intend to make any claim to the absolute assent of faith, and although it is not irreformable but is still involved in the elucidatory development of the Church's consciousness of its belief. Even what in itself is mutable can be binding on us if in the Church's judgment it is here and now the safest, what presents least danger of coming into conflict with the unchanging spirit of the Gospel. Conversely, what is now really binding need not necessarily on that account be absolutely immutable and definitive. A mother, for example, who has to support her children and is faced with an operation which in the considered opinion of all the specialists is necessary, has the absolute moral duty of permitting the operation although she knows that the doctors' judgment may be wrong and is subject to revision, and is therefore not itself unconditional. The Christian must normally adopt an analogous attitude in theory and practice in regard to teachings and moral precepts of the Church which are put forward authoritatively by the Church, even if not as irrevocable dogma. Otherwise in theory or in practice he would be acting irresponsibly, and unjustifiably hazarding his conviction as a believer or his subjective morality. Normally in such cases he can only change with the Church's whole consciousness of its belief, if such a change really takes place in respect of a more precise discernment of the fundamental moral guiding principles or of certain applications of these to new situations.

As such advance in the Church's knowledge must be made

in the first place by individuals, in the minds of individuals, the case is of course conceivable that someone, even while exercising due self-critical caution about his own possible short-sightedness and the opacity of his own judgment, may, after thorough evaluation of the grounds for the attitude of the Church's magisterium at the moment, and after serious examination of his conscience before God and in view of his eventual responsibility before the judgment-seat of the incorruptible God, come to the conclusion that in this or that individual case a doctrine of the Church which has not been defined as a dogma and is therefore in itself a reformable doctrine of the Church, is in fact in certain details in need of reform. Then in the circumstances we have presupposed, he is also justified in his private judgment and in his private practice in diverging even now from this reformable teaching of the Church's magisterium. That does not mean that such a case often happens in the concrete. But Catholic theology frankly admits in principle such a possibility, which follows from the temporal, historical character of the non-defined doctrine of the Church. Twenty years before Pius XII's pronouncement, a scientist and theologian who was thoroughly conversant with paleontology could in certain circumstances have formed conscientiously as regards his faith a judgment that an evolutionary theory of man is compatible with the dogmatic doctrine of man, even though at that time the Church's magisterium still prevented within Catholic theology, by use of the Index, the affirmation of such compatibility. Such cases are also possible in the domain of moral theology.

Naturally it cannot be the task of these general reflections about principles to discuss here such concrete instances of moral theology and to verify in detail whether and why there is concrete need of reform in regard to this or that doctrinal pronouncement of the Church on moral theology in the last few decades. Such a task would have to be the theme of new reflections of its own. Finally, it must be observed that it is not easy and simple in every case to indicate whether some particular teaching of the ordinary magisterium is already a dogma or merely authentic but in itself reformable teaching. This difficulty, which ultimately can only be settled by the solemn declaration of the extraordinary magisterium in a definition pronounced by the Pope or a General Council, makes the practical application of the principles referred to even more difficult.

Development in the direction of leaving matters open

Another observation may be made in reference to "change", whether of doctrine or of law. It is possible, and in fact it already clearly seems probable, that the teaching Church in many moral questions which concern the concrete applications of first principles, will leave the Christian of today and tomorrow more to himself than was formerly the case, and must leave him to his conscience, his own power of moral discrimination. Not that the Church will be cowardly or more "cautious" or would not acknowledge in principle its own full authority to lay down specific moral norms. But because the situations of concrete human existence, in contradistinction to the simpler structures of human living conditions in earlier times, are so innumerable and complex, the "cases" are becoming so different, that a uniform regulation of an authoritative, direct and concrete kind will in many respects no longer be possible, even though a decision in such a situation is still morally relevant.

Just as earlier the official Church could not and would not give any authoritative answer to someone about their choice of a profession, even though it could be a moral question of importance for salvation, so today and tomorrow the Church in many questions, even those of public interest and far-reaching importance, will not, even *ratione peccati*, be able to give a specific answer officially and directly. May nuclear weapons be manufactured? What moral obligation in the concrete binds some nations to give aid to developing countries? How in the world as a whole and in the individual family is birth control to take place? (This remains an obscure question even on the assumption of all the Church's existing or future pronouncements.) How precisely is a genuine relation to be attained in society between authority and freedom? On questions of this kind and innumerable others, instruction on the part of the official Church is undoubtedly more likely to be more sparing in the future than in former times, although the questions, even in concrete terms, are moral ones.

Something similar can occur in the future even in regard to dogmatic questions in the narrower sense. The differentiation of the philosophical and conceptual presuppositions of theological statements is perpetually increasing, and consequently the general intelligibility of such presuppositions and the description of individual positions with the help of a ready-made terminology continually decreases. The questions of a doctrinal and historical kind which are raised become more and more complicated and more difficult of access for a simple, universally intelligible official statement of the Church. Quite recent examples are well-known. The most recent declarations of the Biblical Commission or of the Second Vatican Council on modern exegetical problems may be welcome indications and useful broad delimitations of frontiers. But the possibility of expressing them "officially", in a generally intelligible and binding form, has been paid for by a caution and generality which may give the impression that the actual concrete problems are not really "solved" by them.

On that basis it is conceivable that genuine "progress" in dogmatic development in the future will move, not so much in the direction of a wider, more exact unfolding and precise definition of traditional dogma, but simply in that of a more living, radical grasp and statement of the ultimate fundamental dogmas themselves. A unified, universally valid statement of this kind could be accompanied by quite a number of theologies juxtaposed in a pluralist way, not contradicting each other of course, but not susceptible of being positively incorporated into a higher synthesis. In short, it is conceivable that the "change" in the Church's teaching on dogma and morals may move in the direction of quite considerable "decontrol" and a general tendency to leave questions open. That does not mean leaving people to do what they like, but imposes a greater burden of responsibility on the individual. The same applies to the practice of Christian life and consequently, retroactively, to the importance of canon law in the life of the individual and of society.

There is no doubt that a non-sacred sphere, a secular world, has grown up, which can no longer be so directly and uniformly permeated by universal Christian custom. There is no definite Christian ethos ready-made in the old obvious way with plainly defined guiding lines and patterns of conduct. Similarly, canon law leaves this secular world to its freedom much more than in former times. Here too "change" for the future probably to a large extent will consist in transferring responsibility from direct regulation by the official Church to the individual and his conscience.

Courage to change

In life, law and doctrine, a change is therefore taking place even in the Church. The Church is not a finished, solidly built and furnished house, in which all that changes is the successive generations who live in it. The Church is a living reality which has had a history of its own and still has one. There really is change in the Church, therefore, change which is different in nature and magnitude according to whether it concerns style of life, law, dogma or non-defined but authentic doctrine. Whatever the change, however, one thing endures: the nature of the Church as the presence in social form of God's grace *in Christo,* in doctrine, worship and life. The history of what is enduring in the Church is the history of the reality which alone among social realities has God's promise that it will not lose its identity or die if it descends into the stream of history. The Church is always in the flux of history, not on the motionless bank, but in this movement God's eternity is present with it, his life, his truth and his fidelity. Consequently the Church has less reason than any other historical reality to fear its historical character. For the current of history does not carry it to the shore of death but to eternal life. The Church can and must, therefore, have the courage to change by adapting the eternal which it possesses ever anew and more and more to its own needs. For it is the Church of a world which has increased the tempo of its history to a gigantic extent; it is the Church which is to bear credible testimony, before that world, to God's truth, mediate the grace of God to that world, be the sacrament of salvation for that world. In that situation the danger of too slow an advance is greater than the danger of courageous involvement in change. Its dogma is clear and firm and sufficiently explicit, and the wisdom, experience and foresight of its leaders great enough, to meet the dangers of making changes in itself. God addresses to the Church the question whether it has the courage to undertake an apostolic offensive into such a future and consequently the necessary courage to show itself to the world sincerely, in such a form that no one can have the impression that the Church only exists as a mere survival from earlier times because it has not yet had time to die. But even if it has the courage to change, time is needed, and time must be taken. Not too much and not too long, but time nevertheless. For the Church cannot change into something or other at will, arbitrarily, but only into a new presence of its old reality, into the presence and future of its past, of the Gospel, of the grace and truth of God himself.

Consequently the individual Christian himself must bear the courage and patience of the Church. He must rejoice when he sees that the Church is re-thinking the old, abiding Gospel and is not simply repeating monotonously the old, though true and valid, formulas of its understanding of that Gospel. Even if he must abandon what has become dear and familiar to him, he must rejoice if the Church within the framework of divine law changes its human law and adapts itself to the new situation. He should feel that he has a share in responsibility for ensuring that change in the letter does not come to nothing through the rigidity of his own mentality. Of course change of that kind demands sacrifices from the Christian, too. He must give up what has long been dear to him and do what is new and unaccustomed. Especially if he is a priest, or has otherwise received a good and coherent religious formation in youth, he has to go on thinking and not rigidly repeat the formulas he once learnt or simply defend the old positions. He must strive to feel the impact of new questions, to understand the mentality of the human beings who raise these questions out of the distress of their own personal life. He is not entitled to think that everything is perfectly clear already, or that something is false by the very fact that it is new. He can have confidence that even a new solution in the concrete only brings home more vividly the old truth on the basis of which he has always thought and lived, if he has really been thinking and living as a Christian. He must have confidence that even nowadays serious questions are asked and inquiry conscientiously made, and that people who are not entirely satisfied with yesterday's answers are not always either impertinent people or miscreants who want to obscure what has long been clear. He must really risk mutual discussion with the world, must take for granted that he will not only teach but learn thereby, that the whole truth is always richer and more mysterious than what he has already explicitly grasped, that between the real truth of yesterday, today and tomorrow there exists a deeper hidden agreement than is realized either by insensitive innovators or diehard defenders of the old at any price. He will make the experience that what endures is alive, and the ultimate depth of what is changing is the eternal, that what endures is what has the strength to change. The Church is something enduring of just that kind. We grasp what is enduring in it if we trust to the changes which its own Spirit gives to the Church throughout history by leading it more and more into all truth and into the plenitude of God's life.

SITUATION ETHICS IN AN ECUMENICAL PERSPECTIVE

It may sometimes happen that a fundamental difference of opinion on matters of principle may persist in theory, and retain real importance, while the circumstances of life and action change so much that the difference of opinion is of less moment for life and action than it previously was. It is possible, for example, that the fundamental Catholic theoretical doctrine of the primacy may continue to exist as ground for division between Christian denominations but that at the same time the historical situation will impose on the Catholic Church, with the quiet inevitability of an inescapable environment, an actual practice of the primacy to which non-Catholics themselves will scarcely be able to raise objection. Change in the historical situation may give to an enduring theoretical doctrine a mode of real existence and features which can render pointless the effective objections to it, which were directed against the actual reality rather than the abstract proposition. If on one or both sides in the dispute about a doctrine or an "idea" the historical imaginative model, the "imagery" people use to make the idea clear to themselves, remains unchanged, the ecumenical dialogue advances less far than it would if the new "imagery" of the old idea in dispute were candidly taken for granted. I consider that in ecumenical discussion in the future more regard should be shown for this simple fact.

What we are proposing to deal with here may perhaps serve as an example of what we have just said. There does perhaps exist a radical situation ethics which, because it derives from a purely secular existentialism, is rejected by *all* Christians as moral libertinism. We are not concerned with it here. But there also exists perhaps an attitude to general moral norms, universal in scope and specific in content, which will be affirmed by many Protestants as constituting the specifically evangelical freedom of the Christian man, whereas the Catholic will regard it as an unacceptable variety of situation ethics. The names given to the attitude in question by one side or another do not matter. The Protestant will regard specific norms, in the moral sphere, even in the form in which they appear in scripture, rather as a sort of sign-post pointing out the way to meet and endure the ever new situations of the personal life of faith, with a critical attitude towards oneself and one's hidden sinfulness. He will mistrust or reject, however, specific moral maxims which, by their universality and eternally permanent character, claim to bind men in every situation without exception, on the sole condition that the universal norm, expressing an essence, is relevant to the particular human being in this or that definite situation, precisely because of the presence there of what the maxim in question designates and applies to. The Protestant will not tend to a state in which he is enabled by grace to fulfil the law from within, to accomplish the law by the spirit of love and *in that way* to be free of it. He will rather tend to a state in which he is freed from the obligation of the content of the various moral norms and precepts *themselves* because he can grasp the saving forgiveness of God even as a sinner and while remaining one. The Catholic, on the contrary, will say that there do exist universal moral precepts explicative of an essence, binding in their universality always and everywhere. He will also reject a situation ethics given a Christian interpretation, as being the denial of a genuine philosophy of essential natures and even more as being unbiblical. He will of course recognize an ethics founded on the philosophical analysis of man in his concrete existence, providing it acknowledges calls from God which apply to the individual not merely in a situation presumed each time to be utterly unique, but in a situation to the constitution of which the universal essence also contributes. But he will not admit that the uniqueness of the moral and Christian human being stands outside a structure of specific universal moral principles founded on essences. He will admit and acknowledge that even the sinner can find his way to God through the grace of God. But he will interpret this turning to God as God's gift, in which God gives man the fundamental capacity and unconditional willingness to fulfil God's commandments and does not justify him without regard to an at least inchoatively active will to obey the law.

Our intention here is not to settle this controversy on the meaning and function of specific moral precepts as between a Catholic universal ethics based on essential natures and a situation ethics given a Protestant interpretation. Too many questions would be involved. There would, of course, be preliminary questions, for example the ontological and epistemological question of the relation between universal and individual. There would be questions of biblical theology about the nature of Christian freedom, the relation between

41

law and Gospel, the meaning of the law for those justified by faith. There would be questions of systematic theology, for example those concerning the nature of justification, the validity, and knowledge, of the natural law within Christian morality, the possibility and recognition of an individual call coming directly from God to the conscience in a concrete situation, and the question of the relation of such a call to universal moral principles, as well as many other questions with which the ecumenical dialogue will have to concern itself.

As we said at the beginning, we must pass over this whole knot of fundamental theoretical questions and direct our attention to changes in the concrete situation which affect every kind of Christian morality. They do not, of course, reduce the above-mentioned controversy to insignificance but considerably lessen its importance in practice. What I have in mind is this. The real situation in which the Christian of today has to make his moral decisions is in any case such that in very many and very important instances, the decision can no longer be the simple and obvious application of the principles concerning essences, even if he respects these as absolutely and universally valid. Even on this basis the Catholic nowadays is himself very often, and in the most important questions, in a situation which in practice resembles the one assumed to be always and necessarily present by those who advocate a Christian situation ethics.

Of course Catholic moral theology has always known that there are concrete moral situations in which the application of universal principles leads to no certain, generally accepted and theoretically unambiguous results. This is shown by its treatises on casuistry, its many *Quaestiones disputatae* and the principles it has elaborated for the indirect solution of cases of conscience by Probabilism etc. Moreover, it is aware that there are also many disputed theoretical questions and opinions, so that not even all general maxims meet with agreement from all moral theologians. This simple fact shows that for Catholic moral theology it cannot cause any difficulty in principle to assert that there are cases of moral decision in which moral theology based on universal essences, and therefore the Church's magisterium, are not in a position to offer the Christian unmistakable precepts in the concrete case. Whether such instances are more or less frequent at any particular place or time makes no difference to the fact, which is taken so much as a matter of course, that traditional moral theology is scarcely really aware of the problem of principle which is in fact raised by it.

What is decisive in the present connection, however, is that the number of such cases has increased in a way that we might almost say involved a change of kind. As a result, the scope for freedom and responsibility which the moral principles of the Church and of Catholic moral theology, based on essences, must concede to the moral conscience of the individual (even if they did not in fact wish to do so) has become considerably greater. Even for the Catholic the road from the general principles of Christian ethics to concrete decision has become considerably longer than formerly, even when he is determined unconditionally to respect all those principles, and for a good part of the way, in the last decisive stages of the formation of the concrete moral imperative, he is therefore inevitably left by the Church's teaching and pastoral authority more than formerly to his own conscience, to form the concrete decision independently on his own responsibility. The confessional in particular will therefore be concerned more than formerly with fundamental formation of the conscience, which will then be committed to its own responsibility for the actual decision. It will not be so much a source of information about what here and now is the only correct and legitimate course of action. When here and there in draft decrees of the Council stress was laid on this role of conscience as irreplaceable even in practice, anxious voices could be heard in the aula, pointing out in alarm that in earlier days the Church used to lay down clear and unmistakable norms, whereas now even at the Council appeal was being made to the individual conscience, so running the risk of slipping down into an arbitrary, subjective situation ethics. Those who gave these anxious warnings obviously could not see that today, even if all genuinely universal principles are preserved and observed, the scope for the solitary conscientious decision has inevitably become greater. They did not realize that this fact cannot be met by attempting an even subtler casuistry, which after all would only supply more complicated *general* norms, but only by forming the conscience. Then the expansion of the field of personal responsibility will be met by a growth of stronger Christian readiness to assume responsibility and greater moral earnestness, even, and especially, where the conscience can receive from the Church and the written Gospel no immediately applicable prescription for the concrete decision.

What is the origin of this extension of the field of freedom and responsibility left to the conscience of the individual? The world in which we live, as history has made it. The world in which and in regard to which moral decisions have to be arrived at is no longer a world which remains unchanged during the short lifetime of the individual, but a world in movement planned and made by men. Formerly the facts were there by the nature of things, solid and manageable, and, simply as facts, were the expression of a divine order and therefore in themselves presented no moral problem. And what had to be done in their regard, how men were to act in them in order to do justice to them as constituting a moral situation, had already been practised and repeated innumerable times and its correctness tested, with the exception of a few rare cases of small consequence. People could deliberate whether or not they wanted to obey the norms which had already taken concrete form in fixed custom, but did not need in general to inquire what the immediately relevant maxims themselves were. The way from principle to imperative was mostly very short and clear. Today the world, the environment and the human milieu which the individual finds himself confronted with, has become fluid, because it is planned and made by man himself. Man is changing himself, his environment, his social milieu; he can manipulate himself; he can, and indeed must, think of birth-control; he can, and indeed must, shape by active planning, social orders of greater complexity. Way of life, profession, forms of recreation, possibilities of education are no longer in most cases inescapable facts determined by social and economic conditions, but have been transformed into questions and problems requiring moral decision. The society which dominates the individual is in a certain sense more powerful than ever, yet at the same time it permits domains of decision, and of private life without restriction, which formerly were not available to men. Thus, for example, human beings today are no longer supported, as regards the stability of marriage, by social and economic conditions, but must themselves maintain its stability by their own free decision. New and exacting matters of the greatest complexity, mobility and incalculability in their remote consequences for moral decision have come into existence for men with the management of technology and automation, the direction of human beings by mass-media, the planning of international relations, the adventure of space travel etc. There are not available for any of these things directly and immediately applicable principles of a kind which could serve at once as clear practical prescriptions. The way from general norm to clear concrete prescription has become long and difficult to discern. The official Church can and must of course see how it can cope with this unwieldy world. To the best of its ability the Church will seek for relevant Christian principles but will need time, and it would be pointless to resent this. The Church will endeavour to convey to men more clearly than ever before the great fundamental Christian motives. But as it does so, the Church cannot overlook the fact that the road from universal principle to concrete prescription is even longer than it ever was, and that in practice the Church, by official teaching and guidance, can accompany the individual to the end of this road much less often than formerly. Instead, however, and as the best substitute, the Church would need to give the individual Christian three things: a more living ardour of Christian inspiration as a basis of individual life; an absolute conviction that the moral responsibility of the individual is not at an end because he does not come in conflict with any concrete instruction of the official Church; an initiation into the holy art of finding the concrete prescription for his own decision in the personal call of God, in other words, the logic of concrete particular decision which of course does justice to universal regulative principles but cannot wholly be deduced from them solely by explicit casuistry.

With this new situation, Catholics and Protestants approach one another very considerably. The latter in fact are always inclined by their historical origins to protest against legalism and an over-simplified fixing of the content of direct norms of action, whereas the former defend the validity of general moral principles with specific content always and everywhere. The new situation does not of course simply put an end to the dispute over theory. But this becomes milder, first of all in practice, for the simple reason that now both parties are clearly faced with the same historical task. They have both to answer the question how the individual Christian in the concrete is to be equipped with the insight and strength which he needs to withstand a situation which sets him a moral problem but the correct solution of which can no longer in fact so directly be supplied him by the official Church. It may be noted in passing that the Protestant position described at the beginning has not *ipso facto* been proved correct. For the question which now urgently confronts all could, of course, even now receive two theoretically different solutions. Since only one could be correct, dispute would remain as to which it is. It is also possible that difficulties are now emerging from the present situation for the Protestant answer which were not previously noticed. Life in the concrete was then so simple and sociologically fixed that on the whole it imposed the objectively correct actions, even if the theory perhaps had its defects which

47

were not noticed in practice. If, however, the Catholic now sees that despite, and in addition to, his ethics based on essential natures, he must develop an individual ethics of concrete moral decision which goes beyond mere casuistry, and if the Protestant ethical theorist perhaps realizes that in the new and dangerous situation he must perhaps be less carefree in simply leaving the Christian to his "conscience", then perhaps the new situation will bring about a new climate in which, even theoretically, people will be compelled more readily to think towards one another rather than away from one another, and in which people will understand one another more easily and even gradually unite.

I do not know whether the example was well chosen and illuminating. But it seems to me that in ecumenical discussion we ought to pay less heed to historical theological traditions and more to the real intellectual situation and its stress which is common to both sides at the present day. We ought to think ahead and sense the questions and their urgency, which the age and our non-Christian contemporaries set us both. This age, however (to keep to the example we have chosen), will not be content solely with a Catholic universal ethics of essence which in itself does not touch the moral difficulties of the present time, nor with a purely Protestant situation ethics which is always in danger of degenerating into an empty formal ethics of mere subjectivity of an existentialist kind. Probably the same holds good of many other questions with which the ecumenical dialogue is concerned.

THE CHURCH'S LIMITS

Against clerical triumphalists and lay defeatists

According to press reports, the Council is preparing a schema on the "active presence of the Church in the modern world of today". There is no doubt that very many Catholics will expect a declaration of that kind. They regard the Church as the "light of the nations". They believe in a Church which has the courage, not only to proclaim an eternal life as God's gift and the hope of men, but also to declare that, and how, man has to shape this world of his and its conditions according to the will of God. They believe in a Church which knows of a natural law and which aims at subjecting not only the sentiments of men's hearts but also the concrete reality of life and history to the law of the Gospel. The Church for them is not only the sacramental intermediary of grace and the teaching authority for the true statement of the hidden mysteries of God, but also has a pastoral power by which it can contribute quite considerably to determining the concrete action of its members in the tangible and sober reality of everyday life. For these and many other reasons, it is understandable that the Church feels itself authorized and indeed obliged to have something to say in the name of Christ in the domains of history, civilization, economics, politics and international relations at the present time. And it is also easy to understand that very many of the faithful expect such a statement from the Church.

In such a situation sobriety is necessary. Neither side, neither the teaching Church nor the faithful "hearers", must over-estimate the possibility of the Church's taking up a position on the concrete questions and difficulties of the world situation. This often seems to happen, however, and on both sides. There is no question here of discussing the point that within certain limits even the teaching Church in its doctrine does not always and absolutely have to be preserved from the outset from every error. We are only concerned with the possibility that the Church's official ministry may over-estimate the scope and significance of the *correct* teaching which it propounds and inculcates. The ministry, or in concrete terms the clergy, has often too easily the impression, not merely that the Church has to proclaim what are certainly correct principles of social, cultural and political life, but that by that very fact it possesses, for everything of the slightest importance, the concrete prescriptions which it is only necessary to follow in order to bring about a condition of universal peace and happiness in the world, as far as such a thing is possible at all.

That is the source of the clerical "triumphalism" which was deplored and opposed at the Council. Though it is often not as great as some people think, and has nothing to do with personal pride and lack of modesty on the part of those who bear office in the Church, though it is often inspired by love of the Church and high esteem for the revealed truth which the Church proclaims, it is nevertheless impossible to deny that clerical triumphalism in the sense we mean here still exists. It often springs, as we have said, from an entirely laudable

sentiment. For triumphalists of that kind, the Church is everything, the teacher of the nations, the wise and experienced
mother of mankind. How then could it not be that the Church
knows everything necessary to the peace and well-being of the
nations, that it is sufficient to follow the Church to achieve the
best possible in the life of the nations? Such triumphalists will
then be inclined to attribute all the world's ills to failure
sufficiently to respect and obey the commandments of God
and the Church. They will not of course explicitly contest that
even the pious Christian who holds fast unconditionally to
the instructions of the Gospel and of the Church can still raise
innumerable questions regarding public and private life, of
very considerable importance, yet cannot expect to get answers
to them directly from the Church. Nor will they deny that a
Christian of that kind, absolutely faithful to the Church and its
principles, can make the most terrible wrong decisions with
catastrophic results in private and public life, without per-
ceiving any contradiction between his decisions and the
principles of the Church which he accepts. There may not in
fact be any such material contradiction, while any contradiction
to certain formal principles can only be discovered with
certainty when the misfortune has already happened. But
triumphalists do not notice these possibilities or else they
underestimate them, and so their language and behaviour
assume that false tone of self-assurance and superior knowledge
which repels people of the present day and makes them
distrustful and obstinate towards representatives of the
Church's ministry.

The same fault, but with the sign reversed, is probably met
with just as often among the laity (or among clerics with a

lay mentality). They themselves demand from the official Church what the clerical triumphalists in fact think can be offered. They then reproach the Church when the Church's ministry cannot meet this claim. According to these Christians, the Church ought to have foreseen all the consequences of the Constantinian turning-point and ought not so naïvely to have entered upon that road of symbiosis of State and Church, of Christianity and culture, which involves at least the danger of the betrayal of genuine Christianity. According to them, the official Church had the opportunity of avoiding all the errors and theological rashness which led to the persecutions of heretics, wars of religion, witch-hunting, and all the other dark and lamentable events of Church history. According to these Christians, Pius XII ought to have taken the lead in defending the Jews in quite a different fashion, and naturally in the way they today think could have been recognized even then, with a little good will, as the only right one. In short, these Christians make implicitly and as a matter of course the same claim on the official Church as the clerical triumphalists think they can fulfil. As the actual Church in fact does not fulfil it, does not advocate concrete social demands energetically enough, does not dissociate itself radically or quickly enough from dying social forms, does not stigmatize nuclear warfare profoundly enough (all this according to the opinion of these Christians, which objectively is by no means necessarily false), they experience one disappointment after another in regard to the Church, protest against it, hurt and irritated, and turn into lay defeatists. There are of course some of the latter among the clergy, just as there are also clerical triumphalists among the laity.

Clerical triumphalists and lay defeatists start from the same principle and make the same claim for the Church's ministry. They differ only in their judgment of the question whether the official Church in fact does justice to this claim. The clerical triumphalists affirm it and attribute in consequence the misery of real human existence to the disobedience of the wicked world. The lay defeatists deny it and attribute the real misery of the world, or a good part of it, to the failure of the official Church.

It may be of some use, therefore, to undertake a short reflection on the limits of the Church's possibilities of coping with mundane situations, whether of a private or social kind. Though attention is chiefly focussed on these limits of the Church's capacity in the public and social sphere, what is said also applies to the private domain of the individual, and in fact can often be more easily grasped in his case, for the Church's limitations there are perhaps even plainer and are more indisputably present to ecclesiastical consciousness. The import of our theme must of course emerge from the reflection itself.

Four preliminary considerations

Before the actual thesis regarding the essential limits of the official Church in influencing life in the concrete can be stated, even in respect of the knowledge necessary to such an influence (and not merely in respect of the factual attainment of such knowledge), a number of preliminary considerations are necessary. A little patience is required with them, because their importance for the theme is not always immediately easy to grasp.

1. Principles of action even in the secular sphere can and must be proclaimed by the Church. They must be respected by Christians and are of great importance for the concrete life of men. This proposition is really self-evident for ecclesiastical awareness of the faith and for a real Christian. But it must be stated here at the beginning of our reflections, so that there may be no misunderstanding about the meaning and limits of what we have to say about the limits of the Church in its teaching regarding the concrete life of men. The salvation of men is won or lost in the concrete realities of their earthly existence. For that very reason the Church does not deal in its teaching and precepts only with certain ultimate human attitudes to God in an abstract interior life, but also with the concrete earthly life of man: Thou shalt not steal, not commit adultery, not lie, etc. The Church knows an objective structure of reality which is anterior to and binding on the free decision of man and which as such stands under God's will and sanction. For that reason the Church teaches moral maxims with specific content to be observed by the faithful in every case where the inner structure of reality to which these principles apply is actually present and where this presence is recognized by the Christian.

Such specific regulative principles, which of themselves exclude any formalist situation ethics, even of a Christian type, have also great practical importance. They cannot be proclaimed and inculcated too often or too clearly, for it is not the case that the will to respect and observe them always and everywhere exists. Even if we were to assume with absurd optimism that all men in all situations of their lives are of good will, so that only offences of an objective but not of a sub-

jectively guilty kind against the objective structures of reality
and moral principles occur, even then perpetually renewed
preaching and inculcation of these specific maxims would still
be of the greatest importance for men's earthly happiness. For
even a purely objective and, from the point of view of salvation,
indifferent infringement of these principles produces on the
whole disorder and misfortune in the world. This is because
transgression of the objective structures of reality, by producing
pain, works out as the "revenge" taken by reality, even if the
contravention occurred in good faith. Consequently, throughout our reflections there is no depreciation of the importance of
preaching all the principles which are of significance for the
individual or social life of men, nor is it meant that the Church
by such preaching is engaging in a pointless activity, as if
there were no difference of opinion about the correctness of
principles and as if all the argument were simply about their
concrete application. That is not so. The Church has a great,
necessary and salutary task in the proclamation of principles.
And Christians have the duty of assimilating them more and
more profoundly. They cannot assume as a matter of course
that they already possess sufficient knowledge of principles
and sufficiently serious respect for them.

2. The Church and the Church's ministry are not the same.
When we refer to the Church, make a demand on it or deplore
its failure to act, we very often do not mean the Church at all
but the official ministry and its representatives. If we make a
demand on the Church, we must always examine precisely
whether it is really addressed to the hierarchy and its members
as such, or to the Church, that is, to all of us Christians, and
precisely in the sphere where the official Church does not

teach and act authoritatively. It may well be that the Church has a function and obligation which does not belong to its officials as such. Not all the activity of the Church, which is the totality of the baptized united in faith and love, proceeds so plainly from the hierarchy as to be simply the carrying out of official orders. Consequently when we have to determine limits in the function, competence and possibilities of the ministry in the Church, that certainly does not mean that precisely the same limits are found, similarly located, among Christians as members of the one Church and, in this sense, in the Church itself. The obedience of a St Francis of Assisi to his heavenly vocation was obedience to a call which did not come through the intermediary of the Church's hierarchy, however true it may be to insist that it remained within the limits of the official Church and was tested and approved by the Church's ministers. Yet it was an event for the Church itself, not merely an action in a private interior life which had nothing to do with the life of the Church. Church and ministry in the Church must be distinguished; the limits of the Church's possibilities and those of its official hierarchy are not to be regarded from the outset as identical.

3. What cannot entirely be dealt with in didactic propositions is not *ipso facto* morally indifferent. There is no doubt that some decisions in human life cannot wholly be made available to explicit reflection as regards their moral significance. Probably only in the rarest cases (metaphysically it would be more correct to say, never) is the choice of a profession or of a husband or wife made in such a way that all the decisive and operative motives and impulses are present to the mind

expressly, formulated in propositions, with the relevant moral decision determined only by the motives which are present in that wholly explicit and conscious fashion. But it would be false to identify morally important with explicitly conscious factors in a moral decision. Introspective reflection never entirely recovers a more radical and direct free commitment in the depth of the free being. These spontaneous factors of a free decision not articulated in propositions, not explicitly focussed, not recoverable by introspection, can of course *ex supposito* never be critically judged and elucidated by reflection and theoretical verification, by express confrontation with the explicit precepts of the natural law, the Gospel and the Church. But we cannot on that account adopt an attitude of simple indifference to motives, even to the extent that they are not accessible to reflection. For as well as theoretical reflection on the moral significance of a decision, there are other ways and means by which a human being can either become clear about the rightness and conformity to God's will of a decision, or at least improve the conditions for its correct formation: the general cultivation of courage, unselfishness, self-denial, the practice of the art of making vital particular decisions which cannot be deduced by purely theoretical consideration as this art is taught by the masters of the spiritual life. These and similar ways of discerning the morally good in the concrete, where it is not simply the individual "case" of a moral universal susceptible of theoretical formulation, imply, however, as their converse that the reality of moral good, the scope of man's responsibility, extends farther and deeper than the sole domain of theoretical moral reflection and a casuistry which operates with universal maxims.

4. The matter and circumstances of humanly and socially important decisions have become so much more complicated at the present time that the change amounts very nearly to a change of kind. This statement requires more detailed explanation, because it is what will provide the essential basis for our actual reflections here. Human action has an object and occurs in a definite situation. Both must be known (whether expressly or in a direct and global way), if the moral quality of the action is to be perceived and the action performed in a morally responsible way. In former times, however, the object and situation of a free human action were simply ready-made data, presented in fact with almost static fixity and repetitiveness. With a certain simplification of the state of affairs, which however brings out more clearly the decisive factor without falsifying it, we might say that formerly the object and situation of a man's action were simply data supplied by nature with which he was in contact and by simple human realities which recurred from generation to generation again and again. To the extent, however, that in earlier ages man nevertheless did change his situation and the whole setting of his existence in the long run, these active and not merely passively undergone alterations were so much a matter of "micromutations"—if we may so use the term—that they were made entirely without explicit reflection and scarcely involved any real moral decision. Consequently, people knew what, morally, they had to do. If it was said: Honour thy father and thy mother, Thou shalt not steal, not lie, not commit adultery, people knew exactly what was involved, they had a precise idea of their obligations as something concrete and experienced as identical countless times over. It was quite

simple to know whether they had been fulfilled or broken. And what is decisive, when people fulfilled these definite, easily handled maxims, they had in fact complied with the greater part of their task in life as far as that life was subject to freedom. What did not fall under and was not covered by these simple norms, although falling within the scope of freedom, was so minimal that it did not create any very serious problem, at least in the mind of society as such. The task of the Church was correspondingly simple: to proclaim principles which of themselves could be applied to concrete reality by the individual, because that reality was simple, limited, static, always the same.

Today things are quite different, though naturally not in every respect. The characteristic features of the present age could of course be detected in former times as faint traces, so to speak, because man was always to some degree the inventor and active manipulator of his own situation and the creator of himself. Conversely, the old situation is still to a considerable extent present even today in the midst of the new. Both these facts can convince those who prefer not to be disturbed that nothing has altered very much in the moral situation of man. Nevertheless the situation is different. In the first place, it is enormously more complicated than in former times. And not only when we compare it with the setting of the life of Stone Age men, but also when we measure it by the framework within which the Church itself lived in those earlier times which constituted the classical periods of the Church's life and teaching. The sum of the treasures of knowledge and culture has increased to such a degree that the individual in the time available in one lifetime can no longer have any direct contact with the whole of the benefits of civilization available nowadays and which are in fact known and enjoyed by one person or another. Whereas a learned man in the 18th century could still know more or less all the knowledge present and accessible within his own circle, and therefore within the scope of his own action, today we are all becoming less well-informed, in the sense that the proportion between supply and assimilation of available knowledge by the individual is deteriorating, and inevitably must do so. In this connection it must be noticed that this knowledge, which we know is unknown to us, does not stand in the same relation to contemporary man as, for example, the history of the 15th Dynasty in Egypt did to Leibniz. Within the setting of his life, such knowledge was quite unimportant, whereas what we mean by knowledge available but unknown to us actually contributes to determine the conditions of our own lives, and because we know it is not familiar to us, gives them a threatening and sinister character. Furthermore, the present situation is marked by the fact that it is not simply a given datum, but produced by man himself. Man today reacts to nature as an environment available for his free disposal, as material at his command, so that in contradistinction to earlier times he changes it decisively. Consequently, he sees the realities which he directly meets in his daily life as things which not God but another human being has made by his own deliberate planning. Man no longer lives in nature but in a civilization, in a world which is perhaps very inhuman, because made by man, but at all events in a man-made world. And this civilization is no longer what he produces each time from nature by his own work, but is the prior datum which is the starting point of the individual's life, and without which he cannot live at all.

What is strange about this simple fact is that by it man's situation does not become easier to comprehend and to calculate, but that the contrary is the case. The greater the extent to which elements which derive from the free decision of man are present in the situation with which freedom is confronted and with which it deals, the more problematic the situation of man's freedom becomes. He is no longer dealing with realities which are simple, which cannot be otherwise and therefore can be taken as constituting God's ordinance from which there is no appeal, as the expression of God's own mighty and loving will. Man is dealing directly and perpetually with himself and the works of his own freedom. His situation thereby assumes a character of arbitrariness, of what may at any time be modified because it has only just come into existence, and also of what is obscure. The world of man in which his action is placed, being man-made, cannot simply be accepted as nature was in former times, even where it was mysterious, for even there its incomprehensibility appeared as something divinely matter of fact. The present day calls for mystery-free clarity, because it is made by men. But it does not fulfil the demand, because even free planning simultaneously creates more and more unforeseen factors, brings about situations with which the planner had not reckoned, simply because even the subtlest planning must always and will always have to reckon with an unplanned and not wholly intelligible material and because the planning itself even in the future will never originate from a single planner but will perpetually come into ever greater conflict with the plans of others which have not been taken into account. Through the rationalization of human existence the irrational does not really diminish. On the contrary, it increases faster than what is rationalized, by the very fact that with each plan the unrationalizable residue, together with the remote effects of the planning, involves more and more consequences. The irrationality of nuclear weapons is greater than that of the old knives and cannon.

To the extent that the man-made setting of man's life and the setting which was naturally antecedent to human freedom are specifically different, the latter being characteristic of earlier times and the former of the present, we are now living in a setting which almost in its very essence is more complicated and intractable and inaccessible to the understanding of the individual than was ever the case before.

Universal doctrine and individual decision

On these assumptions the following must now be said if the limits of the influence exerted by the Church as ministry are to be clearly recognized. The distance between the moral principles which the Church proclaims and—leaving aside for the moment the question of the Church's pastoral office— which alone can be propounded doctrinally, and the concrete prescriptions by which the individual and the various human communities freely shape their existence, has now increased to an extent that introduces what is practically a difference of nature as compared with earlier times. Of course there has always been a gap between general principles, which state what is fundamental and universal, and concrete prescriptions which aim at something individual here and now. It is the distance between the abstract concept and concrete reality, between reason which as such can grasp expressly only what is universal or the universal in the individual, and freedom which concerns and brings about the individual as such. To that extent there has always been this distance, this anthropological difference. The Church was always only able to proclaim universal moral principles; where the Christian acted as bound by the teaching of the Church, he always had to keep his action within the framework of the principles of natural law and of the Gospel which were taught by the Church. And certainly by that, in a situation which was a ready-made and easily grasped datum, a quite definite concrete action was in fact imposed in innumerable cases which covered the greater part of his life.

But even in those earlier times the difference we are concerned with existed in principle and was quite perceptibly felt in individual and social life. Even in those days the official Church could give the individual no unequivocal concrete information about the choice of a profession or the choice of a wife or husband. In very many instances in actual life the Church had to leave the individual to his own conscience, even though it was neither easy nor sure for the individual to draw from general Christian principles a concrete prescription for a definite course of action at a definite point of space and time in his life. And neither the individual Christian nor the Church regarded this handing over of responsibility to the individual conscience for the concrete decision as exceptional or dangerous. It was probably only in the rarest cases that the Church in earlier times officially adopted a particular attitude to definite practical questions in the field of politics, culture and economics, although these were of great consequence for human societies and could involve much misfortune. For the most part the Church was silent and limited itself quite serenely to proclaiming very general principles of political, cultural and economic life. Even the differences of opinion among moral theologians, sometimes very considerable differences, which were tolerated by the Church for centuries and not settled by a doctrinal pronouncement, especially on points where it was a question of an attempt to give concrete form to general moral principles, show that the difference we are concerned with has always existed to some extent and therefore does not involve an absolutely new situation for the Church today.

Once again, however, this does not exclude but on the contrary includes the fact that in earlier times the difference was considerably smaller, that it made itself much less felt in human and Christian life as a whole. Consequently it scarcely represented a problem that was really experienced as fundamental. At the most it was one when philosophers and theologians disputed about the precise relation between universals and concrete particulars. That controversy over universals had, however, no practical significance for the life of the Church or of the individual Christian.

Today the situation is different. The difference between the general moral principles taught by the Church and concrete reality is everywhere perceptible and constitutes an extraordinarily difficult state of affairs for the Church and the individual Christian. It is not that the general principles are no longer valid, unimportant or should be replaced by a situation ethics because they are of no consequence. Nor are we concerned here with the gap between the principles taught by the Church and the actual respect shown to them. It has already been emphasized that that is not our subject. In fact it could with justice be said that the principles are all the more important as ultimate orientation and guides, the more complicated, obscure and inaccessible to total conscious analysis the reality becomes which man himself creates and in which he must morally subsist. The difference is nevertheless almost so much greater now as to be of a different kind. It is directly tangible everywhere, painful and menacing. The reason has already been indicated. The subject-matter and circumstances of important human and social decisions have increased in complexity to such an extent that the whole context has practically changed its nature.

Reflection on general principles, the further and to a certain extent always possible elaboration of such principles in the direction of greater concreteness cannot in principle keep pace with the increasing complexity of subject-matter and circumstances of individual and social decisions. The gap irresistibly widens. The causes of the inevitability of the growth of this difference cannot be gone into in detail here. We shall only point out that the greater the area of freedom which man actively makes for himself, the more incalculable that area of freedom becomes, because it brings with it new and fluid situations which are only thoroughly analysed when they already belong to the past.

It must not be overlooked that because the Church has to announce a revelation which came to an end with the apostles, it is engaged in a history of reflection on the natural law committed to its care. That history is not at an end and is only accomplished in connection with concrete events. The

Church necessarily experiences a gap between the general principles which it transmits from apostolic tradition or which it first has to formulate by express reflection as part of the history of recognition of the natural law, and the new concrete realities which emerge in the history of its members. Only someone who had an absolutely unhistorical conception of the way men come to discover truth could imagine that men can respond immediately to every new situation that arises with a concrete application of their general principles to the situation. Only someone who overlooks the fact that this answer itself has a real history which is a history of the reality reflected on as well as of the reflection itself, can think that the Church with its principles, because they too can be given concrete form, is always able to follow directly on the heels of what is new in the changing course of history and that only by its own fault and failure could the Church lag behind events in its theological reflection on morals. In many respects it was only possible to speak with full theological accuracy about the Constantinian turning-point, the feudal State of the Middle Ages and innumerable other events in the life of the Church, when these events already belonged to the past. In principle there are innumerable realities in regard to which we can only really become wise by experience, and so actually never can. For when the damage is done, the things in question are already past and gone.

But let us leave epistemological considerations of a fundamental kind regarding the inevitability of that gap. Let it suffice to indicate the fact that a difference has become greater and is becoming ever greater, and then try to illustrate it by a few examples. The Church can lay down basic principles for the organization of economic life. The Church does so, and these principles are certainly very important and very fruitful, and to transgress them can have catastrophic consequences. But the Church cannot offer a concrete model of the economy as it might be today and as in certain circumstances it ought to be, in such a way that to realize this model would be a binding moral duty on those in charge of economic life. The general principles of the Church on the abstract theoretical level admit of realization in various concrete models of an economy. Yet in a certain situation one particular model among these models, all of which are legitimate on general principles, may be the only correct one effectively to achieve the humane purpose of an economic order. Or it may be the model which alone is to be chosen in a certain historical decision if an economy is not to be damaged by a chaos of opposing tendencies, even if the model in question were not the only factually and therefore morally correct one objectively imposed by the actual situation itself prior to a free historical decision. Now the Church cannot determine in official pronouncements which of these numerous models is in one or other of these senses the correct one. And yet the answer to such a question can be a matter of life and death for a civilization or for the whole world. Nor can it be said that such a choice is shown to be morally indifferent by the very fact that it cannot definitively be regulated even by a pronouncement of the Church's magisterium and that it is merely a question of greater or less earthly happiness without moral relevance. Such an opinion would presuppose the false theory that all that is moral is susceptible as such of being brought completely and explicitly before the mind by reflection. No one can deny that the difference between the moral principles of the economic order and the concrete model of an economy which ought to exist today, is becoming greater and greater. It is not that those principles are contradicted by the actual concrete economy—that is not the question at the moment—but the formal abstract character of the principles is becoming increasingly evident, and so is the fact that a concrete model and a clear guide for practical action cannot be derived from them.

The case is similar, as probably no one will really deny, in the domains of social policy, culture and education, in the attitude of Christians to thermo-nuclear and other modern weapons and in innumerable similar questions of public life at the present day. Everywhere even earnest Christians, unconditionally devoted to the teaching of the Church, are quite emphatically in disagreement on such matters, as soon as the attempt is made to pass from general principles to a concrete prescription. In most instances the Church is at pains not to adopt a definite attitude. The ultimate reason is not cowardice or unprincipled oscillation between old and new, or mere tactics, but the realization, even if not a fully explicit one, that the Church in principle cannot in most instances adopt a definite attitude. For the difference between concrete and universal is itself impossible to abolish. Moreover, it has almost changed its nature today because in human life it has widened so enormously, whereas the Church, being simply the teacher of the universal natural law and of apostolic tradition, cannot do more than proclaim general principles.

Of course in virtue of its pastoral office the Church can also certainly give concrete instructions which are prescriptions and not merely principles, primarily in the domain of the Church's own life. Furthermore, the Church, in accordance with its doctrine, can certainly also regulate by prescriptions and not only by principles the conscience of the faithful. For the Church can negatively proscribe definite concrete modes of action, social institutions etc., as incompatible *in concreto* with its universal maxims. For example, the Church may forbid membership of a particular political party, secret society and so on. But that does not decide the question to what extent such a negative operation of the Church's pastoral office, which goes beyond its teaching authority, must necessarily be objectively correct in any individual instance. Nor does it tell us whether such a negative concrete instruction can be translated back again into a fundamental principle of a positive kind. And what is the source of this right of the Church to issue negative precepts? What limits has it as a consequence? What *special* possibility can there remain in such cases for the conscience of an individual who thinks otherwise, and who in our hypothesis cannot help thinking otherwise, without his becoming *ipso facto* a schismatic? To what extent is such an instruction of the Church, which by the very nature of the case is determined by certain conditions of its time, not rendered obsolete by a change of circumstances, even without an express declaration of the Church?

Above all, such a negative function of the pastoral office does not of itself mean that the Church can, through its pastoral office if not its magisterium, issue always and everywhere positive concrete prescriptions for the concrete life of the individual and of society. The Church not only does not do so, the Church cannot do so, for the Church would be going beyond what is possible to it. The contention that the Church ought to do so, or the complaint that it does not, are both false in principle. That does not mean that these limits can never actually be overstepped either way, by too little or too much official decision and pronouncement by the Church.

For the professional theologian a further observation may be added. We know that in what has been said, we have not taken into account all the possible objections to our thesis which could be drawn from the Church's pastoral office or from certain marginal phenomena of the Church's doctrinal magisterium. It could be pointed out that the Church's magisterium can establish what are termed "dogmatic facts", that the Church can infallibly know that a particular human being is in heaven, and so on. It is impossible to go into all these objections here. Only this can be said: The fact that throughout its whole history and in innumerable cases of intrinsically incalculable importance for the well-being of men, the Church has given no concrete binding judgment (who is the unjust aggressor in a particular war; which concrete social tendency is the correct one; what kind of colonialism is permissible, and what precise kind is immoral; what particular mode of education truly forms human beings, which in the long run does not do so sufficiently; what *apertura a sinistra* is necessary and salutary, which is a deadly danger for a community and so on) shows that the Church in principle *cannot* do that kind of thing, at least in most cases. For otherwise the Church would have acted against its duty and capacity in a way and to an extent which the theologian cannot ascribe to a Church which as a whole is indefectible in the love of God and not only in its truth. In very many cases what is called the

Church's failure to act is an absence of competence for which the Church cannot be blamed. For example, the Church need not have any greater foresight into the future than is possible to the normal average decent person. And the few more clear-sighted prophets there may also be in the world need not necessarily be found among the Church's ministers and may perhaps have to preach to that ministry in vain.

It follows from what has been said that the clerical triumphalism and the lay defeatism mentioned at the beginning are equally false. They both spring from an exaggerated view of the possibilities of the Church's ministry, both in regard to the magisterium and the pastoral office, and particularly in respect of our present historical situation. If a common root is sought for these two false attitudes, the over-estimation of the Church's possibilities of directly shaping the world is founded on an underestimation of the Church's own proper function. Both the lay defeatists, who lament that the Church pitiably lags behind its present day task, fails to act and time and time again backs the wrong horse, and the clerical triumphalists, who proclaim with ardent enthusiasm the principles of the Church and think that the *mondo megliore* would radiantly dawn provided these principles were generally accepted, underestimate theoretically and existentially the proper, religious function of the Church. That the Lord's Supper is celebrated and his death proclaimed until he returns; that in the name of the triune God baptism is administered and God's justifying Word is preached; that we are the Lord's in life and in death and therefore in our first and in our last failure; that we believe, hope and love—to proclaim and mediate *that* is the proper function of the Church.

Certainly Christian life, which is nothing other than the acceptance of the ineffable mystery of God as love, must be accomplished in the concrete details of earthly life, which is determined by the secular forces of science, of politics, of power and also of guilt. Certainly the Christian life which the Church has to mediate is not a ghetto-like idyll carefully safeguarded and cultivated in the margin of the rest of life, solely in the gentle inwardness of conscience or in the respectable Sunday churchgoing of a family seen as the last oasis in the omnipotence of a pitiless new age. The grey harshness of everyday economic and political life, of the most secular research, of that art which is not addressing explicit hymns to God, in short, the secular world itself is the stage and the material and the genuine objectivation of Christian existence and life. In comparison with it, what is expressly Christian and ecclesiastical in profession of faith, prayer and worship occupies quite justifiably in time and quantity a relatively modest proportion of people's lives. It is of course true that the expressly Christian and ecclesiastical elements are of irreplaceable importance as objective expressions of a grace which is incarnational in structure, and as a source of strength to endure the secular world as a Christian vocation. But for this Christianity in the world itself, the decisive task of the Church is definitely not a facile preparation of concrete patterns for such a Christian life, of such a kind that it would only be necessary to copy them obediently, conscientiously and comfortably for one to be *ipso facto* a good Christian. For that life the Church does not offer patterns, but strength to endure it even without patterns, and it offers this strength precisely by fulfilling the religious function which properly belongs to it.

If by the power of God's grace we are in a position to accept ourselves as pilgrims, as mortal men seeking their way with difficulty through the darkness, as failing again and again and yet bound in duty to an earthly task; if the Church effects that acceptance by celebrating the death of the Lord, and makes us men of prayer who are really conscious of the future judgment of God, if the Church sends its children strengthened with God's grace out into their own maturity which burdens them but sets them free, then the Church by its official ministry has done what it alone can and must do. If we understand these limits of the Church which at bottom are its strength, because the Church is ultimately the Church of the Gospel and of the liberating and merciful grace of God and not the Church of an ever more detailed and minutely differentiated law, then we shall be more moderate both in praising what the Church's ministry can directly achieve for the earthly well-being of the world and in blaming it for its manifold failure.

All that has been said about the limits of the Church's ministry in the concrete shaping of the world must not itself be regarded as a formula with the help of which all problems regarding criticism of the Church can be solved. Even if what has been said is found acceptable, differences of opinion may persist about various particular questions of history and the day to day life of the Church, and in fact remain insoluble, and therefore have to be borne in patience. This is so even in regard to detailed questions of what the Church's ministry in particular cases could and should have done and what it should not have done. Even someone who is no triumphalist can in certain circumstances lament that at such and such a point even the simplest principles which the Church proclaims were disregarded. Someone else who is no defeatist may be of the opinion that the Church's ministry has not yet sufficiently thought out afresh these despised principles for them to be likely to be accepted. He can hold that the Church's ministry has failed because it has not proclaimed the principles loudly enough, or has failed in the appropriate calculation of relative emphasis in proclaiming the many principles which often dialectically neutralize one another, or has made too little courageous use of the possibilities of the pastoral office. In precisely the same instance another Christian may hold the contrary opinion, without necessarily being open to suspicion of being a triumphalist on that account.

Just as the various Catholic "moral systems", as formal rules for resolving a problem which cannot be solved directly on its data, do not offer an easy solution for the individual cases, because they themselves are controverted, so too it is not possible with the help of the reflections we have put forward to settle all conflicts among Catholics. In the complicated situation of the present day, we shall very often have to argue in real earnest and bitterly, and precisely while appealing to Christian principles and the Christian spirit. But this can be done in love and knowing in faith that even we in our arguments possess that ultimate unity, through the Church, in what is the Church's real nature. But we should not quarrel over points where it would be possible with moderation and love and the help of a few principles to reach agreement or peaceably concede to each other the right to a different choice and decision.

Until now we have spoken about the limits of the Church's official ministry in regard to the concrete shaping of our world. This must not be misunderstood. It does not mean that the limits of Christians as such in regard to such a shaping influence are located at precisely the same point. While respecting the universal principles of the Church, the Christian by his own conscience and his own inquiry, which is a duty incumbent on him as an individual, has to seek for the concrete prescription by which he will shape his own life and endeavour to contribute to determining the actual form taken by public life. We have in fact already emphasized that Christian and moral responsibility is not at an end by the mere fact that one has not demonstrably come into conflict with the general principles of the Church concerning earthly life.

Just as someone has not made a morally responsible choice of profession or of wife or husband solely by the fact that a confessor does not or cannot oppose the choice, so also, for example, a Catholic at the beginning of the Third Reich had not with certainty done what he had to by the mere fact that by his actions he had not come into conflict with episcopal or papal pronouncements. The reason is not that a moral precept is binding even if it is not proclaimed by the Church with sufficient clarity, although the Church could and should do so. It is because a particular moral action of an individual is not simply and solely identical with the observation of general principles, but as well as this involves something additional and proper to the particular instance, for which the individual as such must take moral responsibility. The same thing of course also holds good of the historical decisions of collective bodies.

It is impossible here to pursue further this difference between the function of the Church in the sense of the official ministry and the function of the Church as the community of Christians, that is, between the Church as a society governed by the binding authority of the Church's ministry and the Church as forming, as well as this, a community guided by the conscience of the individual and by the Spirit. But there is this which must still be said : when Christians as such act, the Church acts in them. Their action is an activity of the Church, not, it is true, wholly directed by the Church's hierarchy, but inspired and guided by the Spirit of the Church. This to a certain degree non-official activity of the Church in the human beings of the Church under grace is an historical manifestation of the eschatological unconquerable grace which God has linked inseparably with the historical phenomenon of the Church as the primal sacrament of grace. It is a manifestation of the Catholic truth that to the Church as such there belongs not only the institutional ministry, but all the baptized, and the Spirit of God himself, that Spirit who blows where he wills.

THE TEACHING OF VATICAN II ON THE CHURCH
AND THE FUTURE REALITY OF CHRISTIAN LIFE

Our subject is the Second Vatican Council. Innumerable people have said innumerable things about it. I do not think that my task can be to act as chronicler of the Council and above all of its third session. What would have to be said on that score is clear enough. Everyone knows what schemata were approved and the main lines of their contents; everyone has heard of the not particularly gratifying circumstances that accompanied the last week of the third session. These were often represented in an exaggerated way—there was exacerbated feeling on the side of the majority too—but in fact they made no difference to the actual result intended by the Council. I should, therefore, prefer not to chronicle the Council nor step by step to go through the contents of the schemata that were accepted. I should like to ask you to allow me to adopt a more subjective attitude, to make marginal comments as it were on the Council's teaching and decisions.

If, therefore, I am to say something to you as a dogmatic theologian about the themes dealt with by the Council, only the Dogmatic Constitution on the Church enters into consideration, if we omit the schema on Revelation, which has not yet been completed at the moment at which I am speaking. Only these two decrees formed the subject-matter of the work of the Theological Commission of the Council, for the celebrated Schema 13 really fell within the competence of the Commission on the Lay Apostolate and the schema on Ecumenism which was passed, its radiance dimmed a little here and there but not substantially affected, belonged to Cardinal Bea's Secretariat, of which I was not a member. As, however, the schema on the Church will probably be the most important product of the Council, as far as it is yet possible to judge, this restriction on the themes I am in a position to deal with is of no great moment.

The situation of Christians in the future

To promote understanding for some of the most important features of this decree (since it is impossible to deal with it in its entirety, and since most of it is already familiar to you), I may perhaps be permitted a small mental experiment. If it succeeds, well and good; if not, I have nobody but myself to blame, and that is not a bad thing. I want to place myself in the situation of an ordinary Catholic of the future, particularly that of a layman, and ask what will strike him especially in that document. Whether the situation will come about in 20, 30 or 100 years hence, does not matter. I am no prophet, and if I am in fact attempting to describe this situation of a future Catholic, as the necessary presupposition of the experiment, then the description is not a prophecy but a dream. Whether it is a nightmare, a blissful Utopia or nonsense, is a question that need not be raised either.

At that future date there will be Christian or Catholic communities all over the world, though not evenly distributed. Everywhere they will be a little flock, because mankind grows

quicker than Christendom and because men will not be
Christians by custom and tradition, through institutions and
history, or because of the homogeneity of a social milieu and
public opinion, but—leaving out of account the sacred flame
of parental example and the intimate sphere of home, family
and small groups—they will be Christians only because of their
own act of faith attained in a difficult struggle and perpetually
achieved anew. Everywhere will be diaspora and the diaspora
will be everywhere. The stage of human history will be even
more a single unity than it already is; everyone will be everyone's neighbour and the action and attitude of each will
contribute to determining everyone's concrete historical situation. And "each" means each nation, civilization, historical
reality and, proportionately, each individual. No doubt the
field of universal history will be very different in quality from
place to place with some parts in contradiction, but it will
form a unity in which all will historically interact. And since
the Christians will form only a relatively small minority with
no independent historical domain of existence of their own,
they will all, though in varying degrees, live in the "diaspora
of the Gentiles". Nowhere will there be any more "Catholic
nations" which put a Christian stamp on men prior to any
personal decision. Everywhere the non-Christian and the
anti-Christian will have full and equal rights and may perhaps
by threat and pressure contribute to give society its character
and may perhaps even coalesce in powers and principalities as
forerunners and manifestations of Anti-Christ. And wherever
in the name of the necessity of uniform education and
organization the State or perhaps the future super-State
determines on imposing a single ideology with all the means

of modern pressure and formation of the enormous mass of men, it will not be a Christian philosophy which is proclaimed as the official ideology of society. The Christians will be the little flock of the Gospel, perhaps esteemed, perhaps persecuted, perhaps bearing witness to the holy message of their Lord with clear and respected voice in the polyphonic or cacophonous chorus of ideological pluralism, perhaps only in an undertone, from heart to heart. They will be gathered round the altar, announcing the death of the Lord and entrusting the darkness of their own lot—a darkness which no one will be spared even in the super-Welfare State of the future—to the darkness of the death of their Lord. They will know that they are like brothers and sisters to one another, because there will be few of them any more who have not by their own deliberate decision staked their own heart and life on Jesus the Christ, for there will be no earthly advantage in being a Christian. They will certainly preserve faithfully and unconditionally the structure of their sacred, unworldly community of faith, hope and love, the Church, as it is called, as Christ founded it. They will certainly freely make use of everything that the future offers them in means of organization, mass media, technology etc.

But that Church will have been led by the Lord of history into a new epoch. It will be dependent in everything on faith and on the holy power of the heart, for it will no longer be able to draw any strength at all, or very little, from what is purely institutional. The latter will no longer support men's hearts but the basis of all that is institutional will be men's own hearts. And so they will feel themselves to be brothers and sisters because in the edifice of the Church each of them, whether holding office as a service, or not in office, will depend on every other, and those in office will reverently receive all obedience from the others as a wonderful free and loving gift. It will not only be the case but will also be clear and plain to see that all dignity and all office in the Church is uncovenanted service, carrying with it no honour in the world's eyes, having no significance in secular society. Unburdened any more with any such liability, perhaps (who knows?) it will no longer constitute a profession at all in the social and secular sense. The Church will be a little flock of brothers of the same faith, the same hope and the same love. It will not pride itself on this, and not think itself superior to earlier ages of the Church, but will obediently and thankfully accept its own age as what is apportioned to it by its Lord and his Spirit and not merely what is forced on it by the wicked world.

If a man of that Church of the future reads the Constitution on the Church, what will he underline, what will particularly strike him? What will he read as an almost prophetic voice to him out of the past? What will be quoted in a future *Denzinger* if only a few passages are to be chosen from a decree which runs to 66 pages?

The Church is the sacrament of the world's salvation

One of the first things that will come home to our imagined Christian is the statement that the Church is the sacrament of the salvation of the *world*. That is found in the introduction to the decree, though the final alterations to the text make it less clear than it was in the earlier version.

That future Christian will be living as a member of the little flock in an immeasurably vast world of non-Christians. How in such circumstances is he to think of his Church? How is he to live with the Church's inalienable consciousness that it is founded by God, by Christ the Lord of all history, that it is the sole eternally valid religion? How is he to do so when the day when all mankind will be Christian will seem to him unimaginably more distant than it is even for us, because no force of a homogeneous society and tradition will operate any longer in favour of the Church? He will be able to do it only if he views the Church as the *sacrament* of the salvation of the *world*. This expression will bring enlightenment and consolation, and he will be grateful to find it mentioned for the first time in an official ecclesiastical document of our age. And when he studies the history of this Council which we are living through, he will be astonished that this statement was made at the Council quietly and spontaneously without opposition, without surprise, without anyone's appearing to notice just what was being said. *Sacramentum salutis totius mundi*: sign of the salvation of the world.

For Christendom in earlier times the Church was the plank of salvation in the shipwreck of the world, the small barque on which alone men are saved, the small band of those who are saved by the miracle of grace from the *massa damnata,* and the *extra ecclesiam nulla salus* was understood in a very exclusive and pessimistic sense. But here in the conciliar text the Church is not the society of those who alone are saved, but the sign of the salvation of those who, as far as its historical and social structure are concerned, do not belong to it. By their profession of faith, their worship and life, the human beings in the Church form as it were the one expression in which the hidden grace promised and offered to the whole world emerges from the abysses of the human soul into the domain of history and society. What is there expressed may fall on deaf ears and obdurate heart in the individual and may bring judgment instead of salvation. But it is the sign of grace which brings what it expresses, and not only in cases where it is heard in such a way that the hearer himself visibly and historically joins the band of those who announce and testify to this word of God to the world. The Church is the sacrament of the salvation of the world even where the latter is still not and perhaps never will be the Church. It is the tangible, historical manifestation of the grace in which God communicates himself as absolutely present, close and for-giving, of the grace which is at work everywhere, omits no one, offers God to each and gives to every reality in the world a secret purposeful orientation towards the intrinsic glory of God.

In the individual's life a particular sacrament, baptism, penance etc., not only signifies and effects grace at the moment of reception, but also gives grace which roots a man in the eternal life of God even in apparently secular moments and seasons of life. Similarly, the Church is not simply the sign of God's mercy for those who explicitly belong to it. It is the mighty proclamation of the grace which has already been given for the world, and of the victory of this grace in the world. Of course this grace of the world has an inner dynamic tendency to assume tangible historical form in the Church, just as individual justification by pure faith, conversion and penance has an intrinsic tendency to take on tangible, external, social, ecclesiastical form in the sacraments of rebirth and penance. But in the finite time and limited conditions of the individual, this does not always happen, even though justification and salvation may be given him. Grace can be present and operative to an immeasurable extent in the world and its history, without everywhere in the course of history finding tangible social expression in the Church. Yet for precisely all this grace the Church is a sign, proclamation, promise of the salvation of this world.

On these grounds our future reader of *Denzinger*, although he belongs to the small, poor flock of the Church, will have a proud and calm attitude to the non-Christian world around him. He will not have the impression of belonging to a small, unimportant, submerged group of esoterics or fanatics and yet of having to maintain that these few alone are in possession of truth, grace and salvation. This future Christian will regard himself and other professed Christians as only the advance party of those who, on the roads of history, are travelling to God's salvation and eternity. The Church for him is something like the uniformed units in God's array, the point at which the inner character of man's divinized life is manifested in tangible historical and sociological form or, rather, in which it is most clearly manifested because, to the enlightened gaze of faith, grace does not entirely lack visible embodiment even outside the Church. This Christian of the future—encouraged by this statement of Vatican II in the Constitution of the Church and really authorized by it, in fact officially for the first time— knows that the morning light on the mountains is the beginning of the day in the valley, not the light of day above condemning the darkness beneath. The Christian will, there-fore, go out into the world serenely, without anguish.

New understanding of the mission: anonymous Christianity

The conciliar statement of which we are speaking will also make him understand a quite new and profounder theology of the true nature of the mission. He will not anxiously scan statistics to see whether the Church is really the biggest ideological organization or not, or whether it is growing proportionately quicker or slower than world population. He will indeed go out into the world with missionary zeal and bear witness in the name of Christ. He will wish to give of his grace to others, for he possesses a grace which the others still lack, for the explicit self-awareness of grace in the Church is itself a grace. But he will know that if his zeal is serene and patient it will have a better chance of success. He will know that he can imitate God's forbearance which, according to St Paul, is of positive significance for salvation, not con-demnation. He knows that God willed this world as it is, for otherwise it would not exist, and that even what is merely "permitted" is only permitted as a factor in something divinely willed (and not merely permitted), and that what is willed can and must be hoped for, not only as the revelation of God's justice but also as the revelation of his infinite loving kindness to man. Consequently, the Christian will meet boldly and hopefully as brothers those who do not wish to be his brothers in his "view of the world". He will see in them persons who do not yet know what in fact they are, who have not yet clearly realized what in the depths of their life they are, it is to be assumed, already accomplishing. (This is so much the case that we are in duty bound hopefully to presume it. It would be uncharitable to assume less. For can I, as a Christian, simply take it for granted that others are not in the grace of God?) He sees, in others, anonymous Christianity at work in innumerable ways. He will not call their kindness, love, fidelity to conscience, "natural" virtues, which are only really found in the abstract. He will no longer say, as Augustine did, that they are certainly only the "specious vices of the heathen". He will rather think that the grace of Christ is at work even in those who have never yet expressly invoked it, but who in their inexpressible nameless longing have nevertheless already desired it. He will see in them persons in whom the unutterable sighs of the Spirit have invoked, requested and accepted the silent mystery which penetrates all human existence, which we Christians know as the Father of our Lord Jesus Christ. When the Christian of the future sees a "pagan" die willingly, when he sees him accept to fall in death into an unfathomable abyss which he has never plumbed (because in order to grasp God he would have to be infinite), confessing by such readiness that the abyss is one of meaningful mystery and not of emptiness and perdition, the Christian will see in him the man nailed at the right hand of Christ on the saving cross of human life. For indeed, alas, it is not impossible for a man to employ the last strength left to him in absolute protest and cynical doubt, whereas the reality which that man is personally accomplishing and accepting in his death cries without words: Lord remember me when thou shalt come into thy kingdom. Why should that not be so?

The pure transcendence of man's mind, no longer perverted

into a means of asserting man's earthly life, can after all, if it is accepted and persevered in, be elevated by grace. Then, freed from its downward tendency to the finite, it can effect the dynamism towards the God of eternal life who, in his innermost reality as communicable and as communicated, is the goal and end of man's supernatural vocation. And this higher and liberating orientation by grace of man's transcendence as spirit, changing as it does in good Thomistic doctrine the very horizon of spiritual activity (the "formal object"), constitutes by the nature of the case a "revelation", even if it presents no new conceptual object to the mind, and therefore, if accepted, is faith. Why then, in the present order of God's supernatural salvific will, should it be impossible for a man's acceptance of the inalienable endlessness of his transcendence—an acceptance of it not as it is explicitly grasped by us but as beyond any control of ours it comprises us—to be more than simply and solely the transcendence of the created spiritual nature as such? Why should it not in fact by God's action in us be the dynamism which carries us into God's life? And if in fact someone is not given more, not through his own fault but perhaps even the better to ensure his salvation, why should it not be sufficient for him to accept this dynamism by willingly permitting the incomprehensible in its very incomprehensibility to dispose of him? Need we emphasize that in this of course all the requirements of natural and supernatural ethics and religious sentiment are to be thought of as implicitly contained and implicitly accepted? This will be done in such a way of course that, as the experience of pagans and also of Christians shows, a right orientation towards God can be accomplished in the concrete, "subjectively", even where extremely grave errors are present regarding particular specific maxims of morality and religion.

The Church as the visible form of what is already interiorly binding

In preaching Christianity to "non-Christians", therefore, the future Christian will not so much start with the idea that he is aiming at turning them into something they are not, as trying to bring them to their true selves. Not, of course, in the modernist sense that Christianity is only the full development of a natural religious need, but because God in his grace, in virtue of his universal salvific will, has already long since offered the reality of Christianity to those human beings, so that it is possible and probable that they have already accepted it without explicitly realizing this. The future Christian's way of looking at the Church will correspond to such perspectives. He will not see it as something rare and exceptional asserting itself with difficulty, as one of the many "sects" into which mankind is split, or as one of the many components of a heterogeneous society and intellectual life. He will see the Church as the visible embodiment of what is already interiorly binding, as the historical concrete form of what is universal and in fact taken for granted as a matter of course (despite the fact that it is something freely posited by God—but by God and not by some finite being!). The Church for him will represent the nature of man as God planned him to be—his "historical" nature, to which his supernatural vocation belongs. It will be the sacrament of a grace which, precisely because it is offered to all, even where no sacrament is yet conferred, tends towards its own historical embodiment in the sacraments. And precisely as such, that grace is never simply identical with its own efficacious sign; on the contrary, by the sign which it now posits and by which it is posited (both statements are necessary), it gives promise that it is powerful *everywhere*.

If the history of mankind (and of the Church, as the Constitution stresses) is a unity in which all men from Abel to the last human being belong together, and each is significant for every other throughout time and not merely by their immediate contacts in time and space, then the Church is the leaven not only where it can clearly be seen to be a fragment at work in the rest of the meal, but always and for everyone, in every age and even where the meal has not yet, as far as one can see, been visibly permeated by the leaven. To our future Christian the Church will appear as a promise also to the world which is not the Church, and not only to the extent that the world itself has already become Church. The promise is not only that the world will gradually become part of the Church, but that salvation of the world through the Church is possible even where the world has not yet, as far as can be historically ascertained, become part of the Church.

This is so because the Church is the promise of salvation for the world which lived and died before it. Just as Christ in his concrete historical reality (and not only as the eternal Logos of the world) is the salvation of *all* men, even of those who lived before his time, through hundreds of thousands of years of an immeasurable, toiling history, obscure and unintelligible to itself, the same applies, *mutatis mutandis*, to the Church. If we ask: by what is it manifest, by what is it promised with historical clarity and in created, objective form (and not only in the never absolutely certain testimony to grace of the mind in the depth of conscience) to the world of all ages, that it stands under the mercy and not under the judgment of God, the only answer can be: solely through Christ and his Body which is the Church. We accept without special difficulty the idea that the Church was the visible efficacious sign of salvation for past ages anterior to Christ and the Church, when salvation had not yet appeared ecclesiastically although it was salvation from the Church. It will not be found surprising then by those who accept that, if the ages after Christ also fit into the perspective of Christian and ecclesiastical salvation, even though they do not yet belong to the Church in the tangible sociological sense. Moreover, if it is true that the Church will remain until the end a sign that is contradicted, that amounts to saying in different terminology that the Church, viewed sociologically, superficially and as an institution, will always be only one reality within a world that remains one of heterogeneous philosophies. It is in that way that the Church is the sign of the salvation which is offered to all. The Christian works for the "victory" of the Church while remaining aware of that fact, conscious that the Church will never be absolutely victorious in this world. Moreover, he knows that not from calculations but from the word of God. Yet he will not cease to hope that the whole world will be drawn into and consumed in the flame of the love of God, because ultimately speaking it is impelled by the power of God's love in Christ for it. And so he cannot regard the Church otherwise than as the promise that through the very midst of the world's contradiction to God its deeper consent to God is nevertheless being accomplished through the predominance of God's grace. He will not see the Church as an armed camp standing opposed to the camp of the evil one, both on an equal footing and equally powerful and equally absolute, both simply comprised within the unrevealed will of a God who fundamentally has remained silent about the ultimate meaning of this drama. He will regard the Church as the audible Yes of consent which he may hope God has spoken even to the No of the world, and across it, the Yes which remains victorious and has long superseded the world's No. He will always refuse in the last resort (provisionally it is a different matter) to regard the Church as an affirmation which stands in contradiction to what is really meant in the very depths of the affirmations of others, so that ultimately there has to be a choice. He will often patiently and self-critically (for even the Church's knowledge has to grow more and more) say No to what others assert, but in order to say Yes to what they really mean. And he will think of the Church in its true nature as the historic audibility of God's comprehensive Yes to the world, in which God (and that means him outside of whom there is nothing) triumphantly promises himself to the world. He will understand more and more that all that can be really opposed to this Yes of God is an empty No, the nothingness of which becomes more and more evident, for even this No only lives and has force from the partial or total Yes which is in it or behind it, and which belongs with the Yes which is the Church.

Sin reduced to insignificance?

Does this reduce the sin, error, darkness and danger of eternal perdition in the world to insignificance? Certainly not. It is not the case that any such optimism of faith comes easily to modern man—unlike the optimism of prosperous security or of rationalism. For of course he knows darkness by experience, he suffers from the heterogeneity of the world, which amounts even to a physical threat. Men were probably never so little convinced of their own goodness, so aware of their fragility, so universally conscious of their vulnerability, the possibility and probability that their holiest idealism may be unmasked (and rightly) as fear, as a vital need of security, cowardice, lack of vitality. Man experiences his finiteness, his poverty, his vulnerability, his utter openness to question. If despite all this he is obedient to God's word and thinks what is noble and holy of men, believes (it is not easy) that he is a child of God, loved by God and worthy of an eternal life which is already operative and growing within him, he will not be haughty and proud, will not regard what is promised as a matter of course as his inalienable dignity. And if he finds it easier to think optimistically of others than of himself, his pessimism about himself will prevent exaggeration in that optimism. But it is permissible for the man of today to think hopefully about others. And this is almost the only thing that helps him not to despair about himself. It is almost easier for him to think great things about himself because he regards it as a moral duty and the safeguard of his life to think of man in general in that way, and so has to include himself in that evaluation almost in contradiction to his own experience. If, however, he has to think of man in general in that way because it safeguards his own life and is the way in which he can have some hope for himself (which after all is his Christian obligation), then he cannot regard the Church as the exclusive band of those who alone are predestined. He has to view it as a promise for the others, the revelation of what the others are—and if in regard to those others it is not "certain" what they are, neither is it certain that those who are inside the Church belong to the band of the elect.

And that lessens the temptation represented by the fact that so few people in the world are Christians in the Church. The sign of the mystery of light in darkness can only be modest and almost insignificant. The message of what is to come (and that is what the Church is) cannot itself be what is to come; the Church of time is not as vast as the eternal kingdom of God. It cannot be said that such a view of the Church will inevitably hamper or render ineffective the missionary zeal of the apostolate of clergy and laity. On the contrary, it is easier and less restrictive to be able to say to someone: become what you are, than: destroy what you were until now. If Francis Xavier told his Japanese questioners that their ancestors were in hell, and they answered that they did not aim at any better lot than their ancestors, the story really sums up the whole problem, the progress which has been made in actual awareness of the faith since the sixteenth century, as well as the respective missionary advantages and disadvantages of both attitudes.

What has been said makes no claim to have underlined all those factors of devotion to the Church which are contained in the schema on the Church and which on the one hand are dogmatically enduring features of ecclesiology and on the other are likely to stand out particularly in future devotion to the Church. But it seems to me that those pointed out are the kind we were looking for. They present the Church as the

Church of those who as sinners accept in faith the human life of all, with its ordinariness and its burdens, so that we experience our own lot as that of the Church, and ourselves as its members in *that* way; as the Church which is believed because we believe in God, the Church whose belief is not to be identified with what it experiences; above all as the Church which is the promise of salvation for the world which has not yet expressly recognized itself as part of the Church, the Church as the *sacramentum* of the world's salvation.

God's salvific will includes all who seek him with upright heart

All this already closely concerns the second statement which our future Christian will read with pleasure in the conciliar decree. "God's salvific will also includes those who (without having received the Gospel) acknowledge the Creator . . . God is not far even from those who seek the unknown God in shadows and figures, for he gives to all life, breath and all things (cf. Acts 17:25-28), and the Redeemer wills all men to be saved (cf. I Tim 2:4). For those who through no fault of their own do not know Christ's Gospel and Church but seek God with upright hearts and so in fact under the influence of grace seek to do his will, made known by the dictates of conscience, can attain eternal salvation."

Now even to people today this statement seems perfectly obvious as a matter of course. But anyone who knows the history of theology and of the Church's doctrinal pronouncements will be filled with amazement at the fact that it was accepted by the Council without the slightest remark. Ringing in his ears are other affirmations: he who does not believe will be condemned. He thinks of the teaching of the great Augustine about the *massa damnata* from which God in his incomprehensible grace saves some few, while all who are not *baptized* remain in it by a just judgment. He remembers that there have been plenty of theologians down to the present day who by subtle doctrines and distinctions have not wanted to admit the meaning of that text from the Letter to Timothy, or who tried to evacuate its clear sense and force by saying that such non-Christians could not believe because they have not got the historical revelation of God's word and so could not be saved, because without real faith salvation is impossible. He remembers those who argued that such non-Christians, like children dying without baptism, could at most go to Limbo, or who asserted that they were justly not touched by revelation and grace because by their own grievous sin against the natural law they had made themselves unworthy in advance of encountering the revelation of God's word and divinizing grace. Or there was the supposition that they would need to have gleaned something of the original revelation of the Garden of Eden in order to have some possible object of faith. In this case it is not easy to see how such a primitive revelation could have been handed down during two million years. Of course the passage quoted is not easy to harmonize with the absolute necessity of faith, of revelation, and the necessity of the Church for salvation, which cannot be denied either, even now. In order to show this compatibility a very subtle theology of the possibility and existence of anonymous Christians would first have to be worked out on the basis of that conciliar statement. Yet the statement is there as though

95

it were a matter of course, as though anything else were inconceivable.

Here too we have atheism of the troubled, inquiring, seeking kind comprised within the scope of the grace of God. And who could say with certainty that some other person was not an inquiring and deeply concerned atheist but one rebelling against God in deadly guilt? What perspectives and attitudes of confidence, patience and gentleness are permitted to our future Christian, and indeed imposed on him by all this, amidst the radical heterogeneity of philosophies and ideologies in which his life is set, has already really been indicated.

But it is also clear what tasks await the theology of tomorrow if it takes seriously the passage we have quoted. It will have to show how divine grace is not simply the intermittent chance of salvation of an individualist kind granted to a few only and restricted in time and place, but that it is ultimately the dynamism of all human history everywhere and always, and indeed of the world generally, even though it remains a question put to the free decision of each and every individual. Theology will have to explain how grace understood in this way *ipso facto* constitutes revelation and therefore the possibility of faith—revelation as a determination of the perspective, prior to all particular experience, in which man interprets his existence and accomplishes the work of his freedom; a revelation which radiates its light everywhere even in the midst of error and guilt, a revelation which culminates in the historically revealed word of the Old and New Testaments where it has its pure historical manifestation and eschatological finality. It will have to be shown that the other "revelation" may not be dismissed or denied in favour of this historical, explicit, verbally formulated revelation, and that revelation cannot simply be identified with the latter, any more than the conferring of grace is identical with the sacramental conferring of grace. It is still impossible to foresee all the theological consequences of these simple statements of the Council, which were scarcely debated, and not noticed at all by press and public opinion. But they are there, they will produce their effect and promote the growth of quite new attitudes in Christians.

The collegiality of the bishops and the solidarity of the faithful

A third group of statements from the Constitution *De Ecclesia* will please our future Christian. Perhaps he will even be rather surprised about the space devoted to it. We refer to the much-talked-of collegiality in the Church, particularly that of the whole body of bishops with the pope. This is not the place to expound once more the precise import of these statements in relation to canon law. I should only like to stress that on this point the *declaratio* which provoked such discussion in the last week of the third session alters nothing and in fact does not weaken anything of what the Theological Commission and the overwhelming majority of the Council worked out, stated and intended to state in the schema voted on and taught. These texts will be taken very much as a matter of course by the Christian of the future. His bishops, of course, will be men whose episcopal office confers no special social position, power or wealth. It will no longer be an earthly honour to be a bishop in the little flock. Socially the bishop will not look very different from any other official in a small voluntary group effectively dependent on the goodwill of that group. The Christian of the future will not feel himself reduced in stature or oppressed by his bishop. He will take it for granted that in the little flock of those who freely believe there must be a sacred order grounded in the Spirit of Christ. This will be all the clearer to him because of the terrible harshness with which the extremely complicated social structures of the future will have to protect their existence and unity. He will know that even in the community of the faithful there must be those who are responsible for binding decisions and action and that the Spirit of Christ who animates *all*, will be with such men. And that Christian of course is a Christian voluntarily in faith, not a product of social circumstance and tradition. He will feel the bishops to be those whose existence and activity support his own free obedience of faith. And for the bishop there will be nothing left for him, as in the ancient Church of the martyrs, but continually to invite such voluntary obedience and understanding for his decisions, in love and humility. He will have to carry out his office as a service because at his back there will no longer be any, or hardly any, earthly social power of tradition or the great mass of those who will always obey in any case.

Who can tell, perhaps in the actual details of life as well as in theoretical questions, and in view of the unmanageable complexity and difficulty of action and thought in the future, the official Church in its magisterium and pastoral care will simply no longer be in a position to do anything but leave very many things, or even most things which involve particular concrete decisions, to the conscience of the individual. It may even be that in cases where such official decisions still can and must be taken, they will simply impose by the nature of things prior discussion and deliberation of a very fraternal kind. For on the one hand it will be impossible any longer for decisions to be taken solely from above in paternalist wisdom, and on the other, no one in the Church will any longer have any mind or inclination to exercise in the social forms of earlier ages the right—which of course will still subsist, and which does not belong to everyone—of making such binding decisions. It may be that the Church will then observe that in doctrine and practice what is decisive is not an ever subtler casuistry in dogmatic and moral theology, but the preaching of the old fundamental truths in new tongues, in new depth and spiritual power : that the mystery which we call God is close to us, saving, loving and forgiving; that all the apocalyptic abysses of human existence are ultimately those of eternal love; that death is life and Jesus of Nazareth is he in whom God has become absolutely present and close to us in tangible historical form and has initiated the epoch in which alone mankind has found its way quite afresh to its own possibilities and tasks.

The necessary and salutary reflection of the Church about itself in Vatican II will not be the final stage of theology. Another even more important one will come, for which this Council will be seen to have been simply a forerunner and indirect preparation. The ultimate truth and hope of the Church, God and his Christ, will be expressed anew as though what in fact has always been preached were really understood for the first time. The doctrine of collegiality will endure, it will be meditated upon and, above all, lived. But the page on which it is written will look to the future Christian more like a palimpsest, and when he scrapes it the even more sacred characters will appear: fraternity in Christ. So the Christian of the future will read the second and fourth chapters of the Constitution *De Ecclesia* frequently and reverently, but with a slight smile at its rather hierarchical and clerical tone, even when it speaks of the people of God and the laity. Yet he will love them because fundamentally they say that we are all one in Christ, that really the ultimate differences only derive from greater love for God and the brethren; that distinctions of office are necessary but entirely secondary and provisional, transitory things lovingly conceded by brother to brother because they are only a burden, a service, a sacred responsibility.

Growth of the new seed

Have I made too little mention of the Council itself? I do not think so, though of course it is true that very little has been chosen out of so much. But that little holds the seed of so much. The most important thing about Vatican II is not the letter of the decrees, which in any case have to be translated by us all into life and action. It is the spirit, the deepest tendencies, perspectives and meaning of what happened that really matter and which will remain operative. They may perhaps be submerged again for the time being by a contrary wave of caution, fear of one's own courage, terror of false conclusions which people may like to draw. It may seem to some short-lived and short-sighted people that after much talk and fuss everything is much as it was. But the real seeds of a new outlook and strength to understand and endure the imminent future in a Christian way have been sown in the field of the Church. God himself will provide the climate in which this crop will grow—the future historical situation of the Church which he, as Lord of history, will bring about. The Church entrusts itself to history; it cannot and will not be reconstructed according to the abstract schemes or blueprints of theologians, clerical politicians, journalists and impatient theorists. The Church exists, lives, intends to remain, true to tradition and to the future. The Church has manifold facets and is a perpetual enigma to itself despite all theoretical reflection on its own nature. It does not know its own earthly future but pursues its pilgrim way because, guided by the incomprehensible God, it only seeks to be the guide of humanity into the mystery of its God. Yet the Church knows that it is sacrament and testimony, not for its own salvation, but for that of the world, that it serves the God of the Covenant (which is the Church) by permitting and confessing him to be greater than itself, so that the grace of which the Church is the enduring sign is victoriously offered by God even to those who have not yet found the visible Church and who nevertheless already, without realizing it, live by its Spirit, the Holy Spirit of the love and mercy of God. The Church knows that it is only what it should be if it is a community of brothers and sisters who love one another, knows that the Church too must say : If I speak in the tongues of men and of angels, but have not love, I am a noisy gong or a clanging cymbal.